CORPORATE WORSHIP
IN THE
REFORMED TRADITION

Books by James Hastings Nichols
Published by The Westminster Press

CORPORATE WORSHIP
IN THE REFORMED TRADITION

DEMOCRACY AND THE CHURCHES

*By Robert Hastings Nichols
and James Hastings Nichols*

PRESBYTERIANISM IN NEW YORK STATE:
A History of the Synod and Its Predecessors

CORPORATE WORSHIP
IN THE
REFORMED TRADITION

by
James Hastings Nichols

WIPF & STOCK · Eugene, Oregon

Scripture quotations from the Revised Standard Version of the Bible are copyright, 1946 and 1952, by the Division of Christian Education of the National Council of Churches, and are used by permission.

Wipf and Stock Publishers
199 W 8th Ave, Suite 3
Eugene, OR 97401

Corporate Worship in the Reformed Tradition
By Nichols, James Hastings
Copyright©1968 Westminster John Knox Press
ISBN 13: 978-1-62564-807-5
Publication date 4/14/2014
Previously published by Westminster John Knox Press, 1968

CONTENTS

Foreword 7
I. The Intent of the Reformers 11
II. The Essentials of the Reformed Service 29
III. The Mass Reformed 52
IV. Preaching and Communion Orders Reformed 71
V. Puritanism and the Anti-liturgical Movement 90
VI. Pietism and Evangelicalism: The Experience of Conversion 111
VII. Moralism, Rationalist or Sentimental 134
VIII. Catholic Traditionalism 152
Epilogue: Heritage and Vocation 171
Notes 177
Index 183

FOREWORD

In 1956 the author delivered the Sprunt Lectures at Union Theological Seminary in Richmond, Virginia, on "Worship in the Reformed Tradition." Before they were published Dr. Howard Hageman's Stone Lectures of 1960 on the same topic appeared as *Pulpit and Altar* (John Knox Press, 1962). It seemed advisable, consequently, to delay publication of the Sprunt lectures further until they could be developed substantially. The publication of *Christ and Architecture: Building Presbyterian/Reformed Churches*, by Donald J. Bruggink and Carl H. Droppers (Wm. B. Eerdmans Publishing Company, 1965), has made the original Sprunt lecture on church architecture superfluous. The five other lectures of the original series have been almost doubled in the chapters that follow, consisting of studies on selected phases or movements of the history.

The term "Reformed" perhaps requires some explanation since it is not widely used in English in such a comprehensive sense as here. The Reformed churches of the European Continent present no problem, but where is the Reformed tradition in the English-speaking world? The great schism of English Protestantism of 1662 left a series of denominations, distinguished among themselves especially by forms of polity and more conscious of minor domestic distinctions than of the basic theological issues with other types of Christianity. To the Lutheran or

Roman Catholic immigrants of the nineteenth century to the United States they all seemed to be "Reformed" or Puritan, and in considerable measure this was true in a historical and ecumenical perspective. Even Methodism largely fits the type, despite its traditional feud with "Calvinism." High Church Episcopalians at one end of the scale, to be sure, and doctrinaire defenders of congregational autonomy at the other are not to be so classified. The family of related denominations, however—Episcopalian, Methodist, Presbyterian, Congregational, Baptist, Disciple—may be called "Reformed" in a loose sense for want of a better term. In any case, such is the scope of this survey.

Another more pragmatic criterion of inclusion has largely coincided with the classification by ethos and theology. There is a substantial literature on the history of liturgy for those bodies, especially Lutheran and Episcopalian, which have a full authorized literary expression. Comparatively little attention has been given to the worship of other traditions, and what there is tends to be dominated by literary rather than liturgical criteria. The history of Anglican worship, much of which belongs here on theological and historical grounds, has been treated in more summary fashion than the rest because it has been so extensively discussed.

"Worship" in this book focuses on the regular Lord's Day worship, services of preaching and Holy Communion, with some reference to weekday worship. There are other aspects of worship that could not be treated in these dimensions. An adequate account of the forms and practices of Baptism, nurture, admission to Communion, on the one hand, and of discipline, excommunication, and restoration, on the other, would have doubled the proportions. The practices and literature of private devotion and the expressions of religious art, especially architecture and music, would also belong in any comprehensive study.

Foreword

A number of debatable assumptions will be perceived in the presentation. The recognition of the cultural relativity of forms of worship is more thoroughgoing than is often the case, and the refusal to admit the abstraction of cult from the whole Christian life of the community in question, its social structure, its faith, its discipline and practice. Considerable attention is paid to the changing balance of function in public worship, whether evangelistic, educational, or expressive, as well as that between the felt existential concerns of the local congregation and the sense of shared heritage with the church catholic of all times and places.

Help and stimulation have been received from students and colleagues in several institutions, as well as from many authors whose traces will be noticed even when they are not acknowledged. Some of the additional materials were presented in lecture form at the Divinity School of the University of Chicago, at the summer session of Union Theological Seminary in New York, at Asbury Theological Seminary, at Princeton Theological Seminary, and elsewhere. The patience and encouragement shown by President James A. Jones, the Trustees and Faculty, of Union Theological Seminary in Richmond are gratefully acknowledged. Professor Leonard J. Trinterud read the manuscript critically, and his observations and suggestions have been most valuable. A special debt is due Dr. Alexander St. Ivanyi for his guidance in Hungarian history.

J. H. N.

I
THE INTENT
OF THE REFORMERS

IN THE LONG HISTORY OF THE WORSHIPING CHRISTIAN community, or at least of the Latin-speaking section of it, the sixteenth century witnessed the most momentous changes since the days of Gregory the Great in the sixth century. The intervening millennium, in fact, may be regarded in the perspectives set by the Second Vatican Council as a liturgical parenthesis, defined by the delayed indigenization of worship on the north European mission field. There were understandable reasons for this delayed indigenization which need not concern us here. Some of these reasons also help to explain the suppression of regional rites, such as the Gallican and Mozarabic, and the enforced standardization on the Roman pattern. The effect, in any case, was that a form of worship, essentially crystallized for Latin-speaking peoples by the time of Gregory, was imposed unchanged on the northern European peoples. For a thousand years they must worship through a liturgy unintelligible to most of them. The form of this service, deprived of inner coherence and meaning, suffered over the centuries various distortions, omissions, telescopings, and adventitious additions. Finally, in the religious and moral explosion of the sixteenth century, a major section of the mission churches of northern Europe rebelled. They translated and adapted the Latin liturgy for their own worship in defiance of the Roman hierarchy.

In the five decades beginning in the 1520's, the forms of worship of Western Christendom were radically and enduringly changed. What were to become the various German and Scandinavian "Lutheran" churches produced literally scores of vernacular *Kirchenordnungen,* while the incipiently "Reformed" communities of Switzerland, France, Germany, the Netherlands, England, Scotland, and Hungary similarly adopted half a dozen major liturgies in their several vernaculars.

It is not generally appreciated how conservatively medieval the sixteenth-century service books and *Kirchenordnungen*—Lutheran, Reformed, and Anglican— remained. The enterprise of the Reformers was, in worship, essentially one of translation and adaptation; they undertook very little creative responsibility. They edited and revised in the light of the gospel and what was then known of patristic practice, but the basic structures of their services were almost universally taken from late medieval orders of various sorts, usually combined to restore unities that had become broken in the Middle Ages. Despite polemic appeals to the Bible against specific practices, none of them really attempted to adopt the New Testament systematically as a formal pattern. Traditional forms corrected to convey Biblical meanings was the program of the Reformers.

There were, of course, separatists who rejected all historical tradition, patristic as well as medieval, and who attempted to make a new beginning from the New Testament. Such were the Anabaptists, and later, some of the radical Puritans and Pietists. Their congregations were small and confined to mature Christians, who worshiped with something of the intensity and informality of the New Testament "church in the house." They practiced a participation of the priestly people like that prior to the sharp distinction of clergy and laity effected in the second century. They also achieved a closer correlation of worship

The Intent of the Reformers

and daily vocation than either the Reformation or the medieval Catholic tradition. But the Anabaptists were nearly as far from the Reformers as they were from the papal church. They were as much the heirs of medieval sectarianism as of the Reformation, and they suffered atrocious persecution from both sides.

The churches of Europe that remained obedient to the papal hierarchy reacted in shock. For four hundred years from the Council of Trent the Roman liturgy remained frozen in immobility. But with the Second Vatican Council the Roman Catholic Church also has embarked on a process of liturgical adaptation and indigenization comparable to that of the sixteenth century. It will be interesting to see how the new family of Roman Catholic liturgies will compare with those of the mid-sixteenth-century Reformed churches. The twentieth-century Roman Catholic liturgical movement similarly seeks to correct medieval disorientations by the patristic model, and similarly draws fresh guidance from the Scriptures. And in these revisions, again, the contemporary Roman Catholic liturgical reformers have a vivid sense of the missionary and educational functions of worship: they wish worship to be indigenous to its cultural situation. There is a parallelism and perhaps convergence in goals and methods here which has ecumenical significance.

We have some substantial advantages today over the sixteenth century in these matters. Few modern expositors open the religious depths of the Bible with the profundity of a Luther or a Calvin, but we have an arsenal of linguistic, historical, archaeological, and literary techniques of Biblical interpretation that they lacked. For the fathers of the early church our advantage is even greater. The sixteenth century knew nothing of the three earliest liturgical texts we possess: that of the Didache (ca. 100?), or the Roman order of about 225 as given in Hippolytus, or the Egyptian prayer book of Athanasius' friend Sarapion (ca. 350). Luther apparently thought Tertullian the first writer after the New Testament period. Neither side in the sixteenth century was well equipped to handle the early history of worship. But the twentieth century has the historical knowledge, the linguistic skills, the leisure, to exploit a wealth of devotional forms unknown to the sixteenth century. In some ways we can probably fulfill their intentions better than they could.

There are other ways, however, in which no one else can ever fulfill sixteenth-century intentions. The problem was not merely one of translating and editing, in stolen moments, Bibles, psalters, missals, breviaries, and the like into a dozen or so languages, but also often one of preparing new musical settings suited to the texts and to the musical capacities of congregations. The Reformers also had to *adapt* patristic and medieval forms to suit the genius of their languages and social customs and of a new religious crisis. It may be that they knew more than we will ever know of what forms were and were not really congenial and significant to the young nations of the West. Adaptation and indigenization of a liturgical heritage is a more delicate and difficult assignment than mere literal translation. From the pastoral point of view it has even greater importance. In any case, the adjustment of the two will certainly have different results in our own day from those of the sixteenth century, both on the Protestant and on the Roman Catholic side. This reflection would not have troubled the Reformers in the least; they were not of those who suppose that somewhere there is a "right" liturgical form for Christian worship.

Like those in the twentieth-century liturgical movement, the Protestant Reformers preferred the ancient worship of the third to the sixth centuries to that of the Middle Ages. Calvin, for example, contended that Reformed worship was closer to that of the days of Gregory, Basil, Chrysostom, Augustine, Ambrose, and Cyprian than was the sixteenth-century Mass. The title of his service book was *The Form of Prayers According to the Custom of the Early Church,* and by "Early Church" he did not mean just that of the first century. From a literary standpoint, interested in the language of the texts, he was clearly wrong. From a liturgical standpoint, concerned with the functions of these services in the Christian life of congregations, Calvin was probably right.

The most important point was intelligent participation, resting on full understanding of the language used. Medieval worshipers were, in general, uncomprehending observers of the worship of the clergy. They had never been permitted their baptismal rights as members of the people of God, a royal priesthood. But Calvin knew, as did the ancient church, that "each Christian bears the exalted title of sacrificer"[1] and has his rightful place in the corporate offering of praise and intercession. The people should understand and, insofar as possible, unite themselves to voice the sung and spoken prayer of the service. So they had done in the third and fourth centuries.

Such participation required nurture and preparation. The catechumens of the third century went through extended catechizing and probation of life—three years in Hippolytus' church order—before admission to their functions as members of the worshiping church at the Paschal vigil. All this had almost completely collapsed by the late Middle Ages; Baptism on conviction was almost unknown; confirmation and instruction had virtually disappeared in many areas. The appalling ignorance of laymen and pastors alike, as documented in the visitations of Saxony, England, and elsewhere in the Reformation period, nearly drove the Reformers to despair. Luther wrote the introduction to his *Small Catechism* out of the shock of the Visitation of 1528:

> Merciful God, what misery have I seen, the common people knowing nothing at all of Christian doctrine! . . .

Although all are called Christians and partake of the Holy Sacrament, they know neither the Lord's Prayer, nor the Creed, nor the Ten Commandments, but live like poor cattle and senseless swine. . . . Oh, ye bishops, how will ye ever answer for it to Christ that ye have so shamefully neglected the people, and have not attended for an instant to your office?

Provision for religious nurture was to be one of the most characteristic emphases of the Reformed Church, an emphasis understood as indispensable to its liturgical life.

Discipline, like nurture and catechization, was another essential for the liturgical life of the ancient church that the Reformed Church intended to restore. They did not, to be sure, like the Anabaptists, endeavor to recover the kind of worshiping community characteristic of the first three centuries, in which the determinative though not exclusive procedure of admission was by mature personal decision as over against a pagan environment, and in which a very rigorous, at first almost perfectionist, standard of Christian life was enforced by discipline. The major Reformers all accepted the type of religious community they inherited, in which involuntary admission by infant Baptism produced a community of far less religious conviction and intensity. In such a church the maintenance of any high standard would probably be accompanied by a more pervasive sense of failure and sin than was characteristic of the church of the martyrs. And the Christian life, no longer dominated by the one great death to the world, self, the devil, and by rebirth from the watery grave in Christ, would be seen rather as a succession of crises of forgiveness and renewal, typically mediated by the sacraments of penance and the Mass. It was the betrayal of pastoral responsibilities, on the part of the papal administration just at this point, as is well known, which initially occasioned the Reformation. In both Wittenberg and Zurich, conscientious pastors were driven to protest by the effects they found among their flocks of the officially authorized corruptions of the system of penance by the sale of indulgences. Luther was naïvely confident that the pope would approve his action. The Reformed Churches, especially, winnowed by persecution and exile, were able, in such centers as Strassburg and Geneva, to reconstitute a discipline reminiscent often of the procedure of exomologesis practiced in the third century. As over against the systematic commercialization of medieval penance, they generally recovered the conviction of the early church that the worthy worship of God could not be maintained without church discipline.

The priestly office of the Christian layman also needed the regular nourishment of the Word preached. Augustine had taught that the celebration of the Eucharist should regularly be associated with the preaching of the Word, a principle which Calvin contended for throughout his ministry. The fourth-century service contained two, three, sometimes more readings and a sermon. But in the late Middle Ages preaching had ceased to be associated with the Mass. Most priests were theologically illiterate and could not possibly preach. Most laymen in smaller churches went for months and years without hearing a sermon until a wandering friar came by. This denied them the chief means of access to the Bible. When the Scriptures were translated and read in the parish churches by the Reformers, the people came in crowds to stand and listen to this strange new book.

The medieval disorganization of the congregational life of the ancient church also affected profoundly the sacramental Holy Supper. Preaching had been eliminated; Communion barely survived. Even in Chrysostom's day, to be sure, the ill-prepared and ill-disciplined people were leaving the building before the celebration of the mystery, and in the sixth century a quarterly Communion was probably representative. But from the thirteenth century when *one* annual Communion was made obligatory, this probably represented the maximum more often than the normal frequency. And in the face of the explicit injunction, "Drink ye all, of it," the cup was withheld. The administration of Communion was so rare that in some areas it acquired its own vernacular liturgy, something apart from the Mass.

The medieval Mass itself, deprived of its climax in the Communion of the people, and of its appropriate association with the Word preached, changed character. The central symbolism of a meal was no longer recognizable.[2] What kind of meal is it where only the butler partakes, with his back turned to the guests? Even the table was gone and was replaced by the sarcophagus, which derived from the custom of conducting Eucharists on the tombs of martyrs. It was no longer a congregational action at all; the act was explicitly defined as pertaining to the individual celebrant, whether or not there were communicants. It had become a spectacle, a "Communion of the eye," whose climax was the ceremonial elevation at the moment of miraculous transmutation. The religious meaning for the layman was already approximately that expressed in the later ceremonies of the Exposition or the Benediction of the Blessed Sacrament. The center of gravity was located very differently from that of the ancient Eucharist or the institution of Christ. The radical impoverishment of meaning found little compensation in the incredible multiplication of occasions. The focus was now on the invocation by formula of a dread divine presence, which could be constrained for private use. The efficacy of one such Mass could be doubled by two. The "cancer" of private Masses was, as the Reformers charged, a reduction to magic and idolatry. In protest they led a Eucharistic revival, much closer in substance to the patristic Eucharist.

Even weekday worship was clericalized and rendered impracticable for the layman in the Middle Ages. The

The Intent of the Reformers

daily morning and evening prayer of the first decades of the peace of the church were taken over by the monks and complicated out of all feasibility for working laymen. Here again the Reformers wrestled with the long-neglected pastoral task and produced a solution closely akin to the weekday services of the ancient church.

All these concerns of the Reformers are shared by the twentieth-century Roman Catholic liturgical movement. These Roman Catholics do not yield to modern Protestants in concern for nurture and religious education and discipline, for Bible study and preaching, for the congregational Eucharist, and in all this they too are strengthened by patristic precedents. Some are even hoping to shake Catholic worship free of some of the triumphalist insignia acquired under the late Empire: the kneeling, kissings, regalia, etiquette inherited from the pagan imperial court and bureaucracy, ring, stole, crozier, candles, censing, vestments, all of which would have offended and scandalized the church of the martyrs.

The Reformers did not, we have said, attempt to emulate the forms of worship of the apostolic church. In these matters they accepted, rather, the patterns established in the second century and maintained by Catholic tradition. Two aspects of first-century worship must suffice for illustration of this point.

The first is the Jewish context of New Testament worship. Jesus and his disciples were all circumcised Jews, obeyed kosher food regulations, worshiped regularly or preached in synagogues on the Sabbath, and followed the Jewish calendar of festivals, especially at the Temple, although they probably did not participate in the sacrificial worship. All this continued after Pentecost for the mother church in Jerusalem. There were private gatherings for the Lord's Supper, but the Christian Jews also continued public worship in the synagogues and the Porch of Solomon. Gradually they were forced out of the synagogues, and in time the proportion of Christians of Gentile origin came to dominate. But for most of the New Testament period the basic pattern was Jewish synagogue worship, supplemented by private domestic assemblies for preaching and for the Lord's Supper. Even the Anabaptist attempt to follow the primitive pattern abstracted from the whole Jewish context.

The Lord's Supper in apostolic times, secondly, was an actual complete evening meal for the fellowship, at which the traditional Jewish blessing of the bread and cup was repeated with the new meanings Jesus had given at the Last Supper. The meal, with these blessings and their reference to the new covenant and the impending Messianic banquet, apparently took place every evening in the early years. Within a short time, however, this "breaking of the bread" was confined to a weekly church supper on the evening after the Sabbath, just before the day of the Lord's rising. Presumably the members of the church now ate their daily meals by families. At the suppers on the eve of Sunday, moreover, the memorial actions and blessing over the cup, originally the conclusion of the meal, were moved up to the beginning of the meal, immediately after the opening blessing of the bread. It would have been easier to attend to their religious significance at the beginning than at the end of a meal characterized by the sort of disorders indicated in Paul's first letter to the Corinthian church. The Didache supplies us with a directory for a Lord's Supper associated with a full meal in this fashion. Did Peter, Paul, James, and John ever participate in any other kind of Eucharist? The real break came when the memorial actions and blessings were detached altogether from the church supper, and set apart as a distinct cultic act. This token meal was then moved from the evening at the end of the Sabbath to dawn of the first day of the week, our Sunday. This change of the first half of the second century is perhaps the most radical in the whole history of the Lord's Supper.

The Intent of the Reformers

The church was at the same time organizing its own synagogue service of Biblical readings, praise, prayer, and preaching. In apostolic times Christians could count on the Jewish synagogue for these means of worship, at least for the Old Testament. Their own preaching rather was testimony to the gospel of Jesus by eyewitnesses, or from oral traditions, or as interpreted by "prophets" in the Spirit. But the growing rupture with the synagogue and the inevitable replacement of eyewitnesses and oral tradition with written gospels combined to lead the second-century church to devise a Christian practice of reading and exposition akin to that of the synagogue. When this Christian service of Scriptural exposition was joined to the "token" Lord's Supper, as had happened in Rome by about A.D. 150, from Justin's report, the basic pattern of Catholic worship was laid down. The Reformers simply took over this tradition and made no effort to go behind the second century to the pattern of the apostles.

The Reformers also generally accepted the second-century system of an institutionalized ministry of pastors or bishops to lead the laity in worship. They did not all, of course, maintain all the traditional subdivisions of the institutional ministry that had developed, nor all the canonical regulations, but they considered the maintenance of an official ministry with rules and regulations, such as had become settled in the second century, as essential for the church. They did not attempt to return to the age of the apostles, where the line between ministry and laity was much less clear and where charismatic religious authority, as of the "prophets," counted for more as against institutional regularity, save insofar as the Reformers themselves exercised an irregular "prophetic" role.

But while the Reformers accepted in substance the ancient Catholic pattern of worship as established in the second century, the canonical regulations were not taken by them as equal in authority to the religious realities of the apostolic church. Their appeal to the New Testament was not so much an appeal to an alternative pattern of worship, as to meanings and realities behind these patterns, which might similarly shape other patterns.

The life of religion is so all-encompassing in the New Testament that there is little interest in the art of worship as such, with cultic formulas and proprieties. The first Christians were overwhelmed by the unexpected manifestation of the resurrection, and the presence among them of the Spirit of the Messianic Age. They had been captured by a transforming power that enabled a new kind of life, both in moral achievement and in ecstatic prophecies, revelations, healings, tongues. Assurance and joy dwelt with them, and praise at all times. Those who seek developed liturgical art, in fact, would do better with the Gnostics, or outside Christianity altogether, as with the Isis cult.

This pervasive sense of living in the Spirit meant that the Lord's Supper and Baptism were less exceptional occasions in the life of the apostolic church than they were later to become. It is even questionable whether they were regarded as "sacraments" as that term was to be defined. The Lord's Supper was a "sign" of the Reign, but it is highly doubtful whether participation was always confined to the baptized, or celebration to an ordained minister. It is not wholly clear whether or not some of the meals described in Acts, as on shipboard, or at Troas, actually were "sacramental" meals. And the gift of the Holy Spirit was sometimes associated with Baptism, sometimes preceded it, sometimes followed it. The notion of "validity," of juridically canalized "means of grace," presupposes a later, and significantly different, state of affairs. It seems, in fact, that the apostolic tradition was marked by considerable liturgical diversity, and that what standardization was achieved was postapostolic.

Praise was accomplished with daily practical service as well as with hymns and antiphons. Paul is concerned to show that all the activities of the congregation, prophecy, teaching, administration, charitable service, are alike gifts of the Spirit and acts of worship. The English word "service" is a better translation of the Greek than "liturgy," for it has the same ambiguity of obedience and ministry on the one hand and of public worship on the other. As with Benedict's monks later, to work was to pray, or as Calvin has it, "lawful worship consists in obedience alone."[3] For those who wished a distinctive Christian *cult* Paul gave the formula, which was also a rebuke, "to dedicate your bodies as a rational sacrifice." The criteria of Christian worship in the New Testament are not artistic taste or priestly "validities" but the integrity of service and devotion. New Testament worship, thus, in its variety and flexibility, questions the finality of all liturgical regulations, and by its refusal to admit the cultic as such, it sets authenticity of religious life above all aesthetic criteria. In this sense the Reformers were faithful to the New Testament precisely in declining to pursue either New Testament or patristic patterns literally.

There were perhaps two major religious and theological distortions which the Reformers discerned in medieval worship, and, in part, patristic worship, when measured by the apostolic gospel. The first was that mechanization of the sacraments which undermined the fully personal relation of faith in God. This had begun even in the ancient church. The preoccupation from the fourth century with the precise moment and means of effecting consecration at the Eucharist, whether by the formula "This is my body," or whether by a prayer of invocation, was a symptom of religious and theological disorientation. The enormous emphasis in the Middle Ages on the material elements of the Mass and their essential change continued the process. The meaning of the whole symbolic act in the congregation of believers became distorted and open to all kinds of magical abuses when it became a function of the clergy rather than of the church and was conceived to be efficacious of itself in abstraction. The Reformers protested in the name of the apostolic faith against sacraments abstracted from the faith or even comprehension of the community and conceived as efficacious *ex opere operato*. They had difficulties themselves with infant Baptism on this score, but their very difficulties document the religious motive of this protest. This protest, in turn, was anathematized by the Council of Trent.

In the second place, the Reformers challenged the understanding of the Mass as a propitiatory sacrifice and of the minister as a priest who consecrates and sacrifices for the living and the dead.[4] This is an issue which involves the very heart of the gospel and cuts deeper than patterns of ecclesiastical authority, or transubstantiation. The gospel was the free gift of God's love in Christ to sinners, a grace that could not be earned or merited but that had incredibly been given. Such a gospel was no more compatible with continuing priestly appeasements in Masses than with indulgences.

The New Testament Lord's Supper involves no such conception of propitiation. It is a sacrifice in the derived sense of an offering of praise and thanksgiving ("eucharist"), a celebration of the benefits of the one completed sacrifice by which Christ "has made the sanctified perfect for all time" (Heb. 10:14, Moffatt). The apostolic church broke the bread of fellowship with the risen Lord as a foretaste of the Messianic banquet to come, when there would be an end to death and to mourning and crying and pain, for God himself would be with them. There was here no cultic propitiation; Calvary had made all such unnecessary. Once for all, Christ had sacrificed himself to abolish sin; no repetition or supplementation was called for. The function of the president of the feast was to give thanks and distribute, not to offer or to consecrate.

But this original significance of the Lord's Supper was in later generations overlaid by other meanings. These

The Intent of the Reformers

changes constitute the great difficulty with the notion of an unchanging structure of action in the Eucharistic liturgy, the "offertory," prayer, breaking of the bread, and actual communion of the people.[4a] Is there an "offertory" in the New Testament Eucharist? Diverse interpretations put on the pattern actions "took bread" and "gave thanks over it" raise questions as to the unchanging continuity, especially of the first two phases of the "fourfold action."

With Irenaeus at the end of the second century a new emphasis on "offering" the bread and wine is apparent. This new understanding became the dominant meaning in the following generations, and ancient mosaics show us the long processions of worshipers coming to the Table with their gifts. This lasted until Gregory's day in the West. The "Eucharist" or "Thanksgiving" was accordingly in the third, fourth, and fifth centuries more often referred to as the "Oblation" or "Sacrifice."

The real break came in the mid-third century and is seen first in Cyprian, who, in contrast to his great contemporary Origen, propounded the notion that the performance of the sacramental act was in itself propitiatory, because in some sense the body and blood of Christ were sacrificed in it. Thereby the door was opened to admit again the whole apparatus of Temple, priests, altars, sacrifices which had passed with the old Jewish dispensation. And in the second half of the third century, just before the last persecution and consequent legalization of the church, this reversion to priesthood became generally established. Thereafter a "special priesthood" was needed to make the cultic approaches to a God imperfectly reconciled, it appeared, by the cross.

The Epistle to the Hebrews had apparently been written to former Jews who, as Christians, yearned back to this machinery of propitiation. The author undertook to show how, as Christians, they lived in a new covenant relation with God, which required no repetition of sacrifices after the Jewish manner. Permanent access to the seat of judgment had been opened by Jesus, whose position as advocate rested on his completed atonement, and who reigns at God's right hand and intercedes as our high priest until the consummation. "Every priest stands performing his service daily and offering time after time the same sacrifices, which can never remove sins. But Christ offered for all time one sacrifice for sins . . . and where these have been forgiven, there is no longer any offering for sin." (Heb. 10:11–12, 18, NEB.)

The apostolic church, accordingly, did not have "priests" in the special technical sense. All Christians, to be sure, constitute a royal priesthood, offering to God their praise and obedience. And Christ, having made propitiation once for all, is High Priest behind the Veil. The words *hiereus* and *archiereus* are applied to pagan or Jewish priests in the New Testament and the early fathers, but not to Christian ministers until the end of the second century. As Father Congar has observed: "It cannot be overlooked that the usage was intentional. . . . The application of a sacrificial and sacerdotal vocabulary to external Christian worship is relatively late and at the beginning was obviously shunned."

"Examination of the use of the word *thusiastērion*, altar," to quote Father Congar further, "leads to analogous conclusions. The altar is Christ, or the community of the faithful, or an individual member thereof; down to St. Irenaeus the application of the word *thusiastērion* to the table of liturgical celebration was exceptional."[5] In the building used for worship the most conspicuous furniture was not an altar—they had none—but the ancient counterpart of the "central pulpit," the *cathedra* from which the pastor preached. For the Eucharist a small wooden table would be brought in. The Christians admitted the charge of the pagans that they lacked the usual apparatus and conceptions of a priestly cult. So Origen (ca. A.D. 245) con-

The Intent of the Reformers

ceded Celsus' charge that Christians had no altars. "We have no shrines and altars," Minucius Felix had affirmed.[6]

Luther was simply restating the view of the apostolic and subapostolic church when he maintained: "We neither can nor ought to give the name priest to those who are in charge of Word and sacrament among the people. The reason they have been called priests is either because of the custom of heathen people or as a vestige of the Jewish nation. The result is greatly injurious to the church."[7] And lines of ordination transmitting the power to consecrate and sacrifice for the living and the dead were neither apostolic nor Biblical. The ministerial succession which they overlaid and obscured, of course, had never lapsed, and had maintained the true life of the church. The correlative ideas of a special priesthood for sacrifice and of the propitiatory interpretation of the Eucharist, which established themselves in the late third century, were thus rejected by the Reformers as an unworthy reversion, or to use modern terms, an illegitimate "development."

In this interpretation the Reformers were no longer appealing to patristic practice in general, but were criticizing substantial portions of the patristic tradition itself. Here they are not likely to win agreement from modern Roman Catholics. The Council of Trent is painfully specific:

> If any one shall say, that in the mass a true and proper sacrifice is not offered to God, . . . that it is a bare commemoration of the sacrifice offered on the cross, but not a propitiatory sacrifice; or, that it avails him only who receiveth; and that it ought not to be offered for the living and the dead for sins, punishments, satisfactions, and other necessities; let him be anathema.[8]

The most famous Anglican martyrs, Cranmer, Ridley, and Latimer, were burned at the stake for denying that the Mass was a propitiation for the sins of the living and the dead. This question is at the heart of the issue between Protestant and Roman Catholic, or very near it. It is the question as to how our reconciliation with God is accomplished, whether by God alone, or, in part, by our initiative. Is there any real sense in which we "offer" Christ to God?

In recent years there have been a variety of efforts to reformulate the Roman Catholic interpretation to make it less open to the sort of objections the Reformers raised. There is the suggestion that at the Mass the church "pleads" before the Father the one sacrifice of Christ (de la Taille). Or again, rather than "repeating" or "renewing" or "continuing" the work of his atoning life and death, the priest "reenacts" or "re-presents" it (Odo Casel). Anglo-Catholics have been particularly active in these irenic efforts. The problem is central in the contemporary ecumenical dialogue. Can the sixteenth-century confrontations be transcended, or reconceived, in the light of further Biblical study and greater philosophical and linguistic sophistication? Or do the essential issues remain, calling for decision without evasion?

II

THE ESSENTIALS OF THE REFORMED SERVICE

IN DEFINING INDISPENSABLE ELEMENTS OF CHRISTIAN WORship, Calvin appealed to the "invariable custom" of the early church. "No assembly of the Church should be held," he asserted, "without the word being preached, prayers being offered, the Lord's supper administered, and alms given."[9] This list may serve as a convenient outline in discussing the character of the Reformed service.

First of all, Calvin requires the "preaching of the Word," and this was probably the most striking emphasis of the Reformers generally. Whatever else it was, the Reformation was a great preaching revival, probably the greatest in the history of the Christian church. Riding a rising tide of preaching in the late Middle Ages, the Reformers expanded the practice still farther, and gave it a significantly new function and character. All of them preached prodigiously. In most of the Reformed communities there were two or three sermons on the Lord's Day and several during the week, sometimes daily. The appetite for the Word preached was startling by modern standards, both in length and solidity of sermons and the number of them desired by the congregations. For the twelve thousand people of Geneva there were fifteen services with sermon every week, distributed through three parishes. And although many or most modern historians refer to the length of these sermons as wearisome, they rarely supply contemporary judgments to this effect. Such comments usually reveal more about the attention span of the modern historian than of that of sixteenth- and seventeenth-century congregations.

The "Word," in Reformation usage, meant the written word and the preached word as conveying the incarnate Word. The great preaching revival went hand in hand with the rediscovery of the Bible and its general accessibility in the new translations, as of Luther, Tyndale, Lefèvre, and Olivétan. Men entered with amazement and wonder into the world of the Bible, known for generations to the layman only in scattered quotations and snippets. The preached Word was so closely identified with Scripture that in the services of the Reformed churches the Scripture-reading and sermon are ordinarily referred to in one comprehensive rubric, "the Word." It was one liturgical act to read the Scripture and to preach it. The sermon followed immediately on the reading, and was not separated from it (as in many modern services) by anthems, prayers, and other elements. The reading and preaching were together introduced by a prayer to the Holy Spirit to quicken this Word in the lives of the congregation, and in Calvin's custom, often followed again by a bidding prayer catching up some of the themes.

It was because the sermon was so intimately related to the Scripture that it was possible to restore the unity of preaching, Communion, and prayers without the seams showing. If the sermon is not so related to the Scripture, it becomes an addition to or interruption of the liturgy, or more likely, one has a religious or moral oration surrounded by opening and closing "exercises." But the Reformed preacher was expected to do faithful expository preaching, to present to his congregation the promise of God as found in his text.

Reformation preaching was characteristically expository preaching, and also what has been more recently called "kerygmatic" preaching. Its substance, that is, was the kerygma or proclamation of the apostles as to what God had done and would do in Christ Jesus. The gospel had originally been not a book, as Luther pointed out, but sermons, testimonies of apostolic faith. Such living witness communicates the Word more effectively than merely reading the Bible even today. It is the function of the preacher to make us Christ's contemporaries, so that His redeeming deeds and dying become our present justification. The apostles and those who continue the apostolic preaching are God's messengers by whom his revelation is conveyed to man. God does not ordinarily use angels, private revelations, or even in Reformation thought, private reading of Scripture.

The preacher of the Word is thus God's instrument in a terrifyingly direct way. "I am certain," said Luther, "that when I enter the pulpit to preach or stand at the lectern to read, it is not my word, but my tongue is the pen of a ready writer."[10] God the Spirit, Calvin taught, worked both in the preacher's declaration of the Word, and in the hearers to enable its recognition. Preaching the Word is revelation as much as Scripture is revelation. All that one could say about God's declaration and disclosure of himself in Scripture is also true of his Word preached. The preacher is to expound the promise of Scripture in the worshiping congregation in the expectancy that God will use his words, will act through him to condemn and forgive, to regenerate and cleanse, to console and fortify. Similarly we are to hear the Word preached as though He were nigh to us, face-to-face.

In recent years when such expectations have not been usual, the idea has been revived in the formula of preaching as "sacramental," a term calculated to communicate to an Anglican audience. For Luther there is but one sacrament, God manifesting his mercy to us in Christ Jesus, which he does through the three sacramental "signs" of

Baptism, the preaching of forgiveness, and the Lord's Supper. So for Calvin the preacher's words are "signs" through which Christ approaches men and effects his kingly rule in the world, creating and upholding his church. God's greatest gift to the church is the preaching of the good news which is mighty to save, alive with blessing and judgment. The preacher of grace is performing the most important act any man can accomplish in this life. The fruitful hearing of the Word is the greatest blessing any of us will know in this life. And the church is most church when the Word is preached and heard, for there God is actually calling, justifying, sanctifying his people.

In taking on this "sacramental" character, the Reformed sermon was registering a shift in the whole economy of the sacramental system. To preach the offer of forgiveness and new life in Christ was, in substance, to convey the essential meaning of sacramental absolution, to exercise the power of the keys, to replace measurably a seriously disorganized practice of auricular confession and penance. Calvin, to be sure, like Luther, continued the practice of private confession and absolution on a voluntary basis, and in Strassburg required prospective communicants to confer with the pastor for instruction, admonition, or encouragement as the case might require.[11] For some generations this kind of preliminary pastoral conference was a regular function of Reformed elders in many countries, enforced by the requirement of Communion "tokens" at the Eucharist itself. The conception of the sermon as conveying the assurance of forgiveness to those entangled in the complexities of doubt and moral struggle made it closer in function to the medieval exercise of absolution than to the moral homily or warning of judgment or simple instruction which constituted the usual medieval sermon (to say nothing of the modern).

The central and constituting function of the Christian

The Essentials of the Reformed Service

ministry was thus the preaching of the redeeming Word. Those who did not so preach were outside the apostolic succession, and no true priests. Most sixteenth-century priests and bishops were in this category. They did not and could not preach that Word which should be heard whenever the church of God assembled.

To preserve the consensus of the preachers several Reformed communities utilized a kind of preachers' workshop. The practice began in Zurich in 1525, and was called "prophesying" in reference to Paul's advice (I Cor. 14:29–33), "Let two or three prophets speak." In Zurich the preachers of the city gathered in the cathedral five days a week for their school of the prophets. A selected passage was examined in Latin and Hebrew or Greek. Then its use in a sermon was discussed and finally a sermon preached on it. The Zurich translation of the Bible was largely hammered out in this way.

A similar practice was followed once a week in à Lasco's Church of the Strangers in London, and in the English refugee congregation in Geneva. Here all members of the congregation were encouraged to present questions to the ministers through a committee. In Elizabethan England ministers gathered in certain counties at a central church and engaged in exposition, one after another, of a selected passage. Questions from the congregation were also entertained. These "prophesyings" were suppressed by the Queen as potential presbyteries. But in one form or another the practice was widespread as a discipline in Biblical preaching and a guardian of doctrinal agreement.

The second element in every meeting of the church is the prayers. These are of two types, said Calvin, spoken and sung. We must say something of each.

It is significant that Calvin discusses church music under the heading of prayer. Late medieval parish singing resembled anything more than prayer. "A multitude of sounds is heard," complained Agrippa von Nettesheim of this elaborate polyphony, "but of the words and prayers not a syllable is understood."[12] Erasmus voiced the same objection: "They chant nowadays in our churches in what is an unknown tongue and nothing else, while you will not hear a sermon once in six months telling people to amend their lives. Modern church music is so constructed that the congregation cannot hear one distinct word. . . . If they want music let them sing psalms like rational beings, and not too many of these."[13] The melodies communicated more than the text. For settings were heard "vile love ditties, to which harlots and mimes dance,"[14] wrote Erasmus. Douen reports instances of the Sanctus, Incarnatus, and Credo set to tunes familiar as "Lisette, mes amours" and "Robin m'aime"; or a Magnificat to "Margot dans un jardin"; or a Mass to "Venus la belle."[15] All the major Reformers rejected some of the current church music and it was proposed at the Council of Trent to eliminate all of it.

In this situation it was Zwingli, probably the best musician, both as composer and performer, among the Reformers, who alone took the radical step of eliminating music altogether from the church service. He attempted to replace it by choral antiphonal recitation, as of the "Glory be to God on high," the Creed, or a psalm. Such responsive reading, widespread in English-speaking Protestantism since the nineteenth century, presupposes a general educational level that did not exist in earlier centuries. Congregations did not take easily to spoken responses in Zurich or in Anglicanism, and the usual outcome was a duet of the vicar and the clerk. The Zurich magistrates instructed the clergy to take over the peoples' part and at length in 1595 surrendered to the general Reformed solution.

That general solution, as everyone knows, was a kind of metrical psalmody that made universal congregational participation possible. In classical Reformed worship the "liturgy" in the strict sense, the people's part, was all *sung*.

The Essentials of the Reformed Service

It is not the spoken prayers, taken by the minister, but the sung liturgy of the people which must be studied in the first instance to comprehend the meaning of early Reformed worship.

Calvin's views on the place of music in worship are stated in his prefaces to the 1542 and 1545 editions of the metrical psalter. He assessed music as the first gift of God, or one of the first, for man's recreation. "It has power to enter the heart like wine poured into a vessel, with good or evil effect." In worship, in particular, it "has great force and vigor to move and inflame the hearts of men to invoke and praise God with a more vehement and ardent zeal." A new arrival in Strassburg found it indeed so. "For five or six days at the beginning, when I looked on this little company of exiles from all countries," he wrote, "I wept, not for sadness, but for joy to hear them all singing so heartily and as they sang giving thanks to God that He had led them to a place where His name is glorified. No one could believe what joy there is in singing the praises and wonders of the Lord in the mother tongue as they are sung here."[16]

The act is one of prayer. The music is to carry the text, and not to distract attention from it. And since the congregation is itself to sing and not be displaced by trained professionals, the musical setting must be held down to the capacities of general congregations. Calvin resisted the efforts of the musicians to make the sung liturgy more aesthetically interesting. The basic conception was like that of plain chant, a simple melodic line, with one note to each syllable, designed to be sung in unison without accompaniment. But the metrical rhythm gave a pattern that was easier to master. The tunes of the Huguenot psalter of 1562 illustrate the transition in musical idiom from the medieval tones to the modern major and minor keys. Douen classifies 52 as Gregorian, 38 as in major, and 35 as close to our minor. There are no less than 125 tunes in all. Louis Bourgeois made the most important contribution musically.

As the singing style resembled that of the monasteries, so with the texts. The metrical psalmody of the Reformed churches, in fact, stands beside the chanted psalmody of the Benedictines as the two most notable liturgical exploitations of the psalter in Christian history. Dathenus translated the French psalter into Dutch (1566) and Lobwasser into German (1573), in both of which languages it had even wider circulation than in the original. The Scottish and Anglican versions were more independent, although inferior in quality. The Hungarian came last. Metrical psalmody swept Europe as the most characteristic mark and powerful attraction of Reformed worship. Even strict Lutherans spoke with some envy and irritation of "la sirène Calviniste."

Why did the Reformed virtually confine their sung liturgy to the psalter, at least for several generations, and not, like the Lutherans and some Anabaptists, develop a hymnody also? There was some feeling that one could scarcely improve on the psalter, and in using it, one was praising God, so to speak, in His own language. The Synod of Dort, less permissive than the French Reformed, allowed no hymns. But it is not apparent that those Protestant bodies who first produced hymns had a significantly lower view of Scripture, nor does this seem to have been the case with the Reformed congregations who later accepted hymns.

Two other factors are probably more important. One was that the psalter invited, and in fact received, a systematic use akin to that of the Benedictines. It was sufficiently large and varied to provide a comprehensive and complete body of liturgical song, if systematically distributed over the successive services. In this way the Reformed psalters paid the penalty of their enormous early success. The Reformed had, in one leap, acquired a complete liturgical

The Essentials of the Reformed Service

system, which then could not be gradually changed by adding hymns, but must be challenged as a system.

The second factor is that the sixteenth-century Reformed understood the psalter, and the Old Testament generally, quite differently from their modern successors. Calvin, for example, in contrast to both the Scholastics and the Anabaptists, argued for the substantial identity of the revelation of God to the ancient Hebrews on the one hand, and to the Christians on the other. All true revelation of whatever age is of the Christ, the Eternal Son, including Old Testament visions, angelic messengers, prophetic declarations. The faithful sons of the Old Covenant actually received the benefits of the Messiah's cross and resurrection. Israel was the real church; her sacrifices were real sacraments of the Christ, his life and power. The new covenant in Christ Jesus, to be sure, is clearer, more vivid, less encumbered with ceremonies and cult, but Christ is the substance of both covenants. The Old Testament and the psalms were to be read Christologically and as prophetic of the life of the church. Political and cultic references in the psalms that to a modern congregation seem archaic and irrelevant were at once understood by the sixteenth-century Reformed Church to be metaphorical prophetic allusions to her own life. As early as the days of Isaac Watts the Christological and typological understanding of the Old Testament was so modified that the psalter no longer spoke to the congregations as it had in the sixteenth century. For us to understand the liturgy of the early Reformed churches requires serious attention to their principles of Biblical interpretation.

More generally the early modern age found the Biblical world view more accessible than do we. The Reformed sense of the church as the "people of God," a holy nation, was particularly close, of course, to the Hebraic view of an elect people. People of the Reformed faith shared also a very direct and vivid sense of God's providential direction of human history. The outcome of battle or the incidence of disease were at once read religiously as signs of warning or mercy from the Lord of history. The imagination of the sixteenth century was not yet intrigued by "secondary causes" and had not yet become subdued to mechanical and impersonal analogies for the processes of nature. The Reformed Church, rather, viewed nature, as does the psalmist, as manifestation of the historical purposes of a personal God. In repentance and supplication as in joy and adoration, the songs of ancient Israel read Christologically were the chosen language of prayer.

In the *Pseaulmes de David* of 1562 each psalm is prefaced by a sentence or two facilitating such interpretation. Above the second psalm we read, for example, "Here we see how David and his kingdom form a true image and sure prophecy of Jesus Christ and His Reign." And the book was furnished with an index of two pages, wherein one might locate the psalms appropriate to various circumstances: persecution, temptation to vengeance, bereavement, etc. The favorite psalms were not the same as those twentieth-century congregations might choose. Instead of Ps. 23 or 139 sixteenth-century congregations used by preference such psalms as 46; 68; 76; 124.

As the staple of private and family worship as well as of the services of the church, the psalms became known to many by heart. No other book of the Old Testament, at least, could rival the psalms in the affections and knowledge of Reformed laymen. Ministers frequently preached from the psalms also; the psalter was the only Old Testament book on which Calvin preached on Sundays.[17] For every occasion, it seems, an appropriate verse would leap to the tongue of a Huguenot. And all over France, wherever Huguenots of the first generation were confined, often sometimes by the score, guards and jailers became familiar with the psalms, even to prisons on Santo Domingo and Martinique. The colporteurs who carried the psalters, with Bibles and catechisms, all over France, were frequently

The Essentials of the Reformed Service

caught and burned. Many martyrs died with the words of the Apostles' Creed, but it is surprising to see what a range of the psalter was drawn on by others.

The courage and joy of these martyrs who, like the ancient Christians, could have had release for a word, won converts among the onlookers. The authorities tried gags, but the cord would burn and from out of the smoke the psalm would again begin. The bishops then ordered that the tongues of the Huguenots should be cut out before they were burned. This became the general practice. At Orange, pieces were torn from the Bible and psalters and forced into the mouths and wounds of the victims. "Eat your fill; tell your God to come rescue you."[18]

When the fifty-seven Protestants of Meaux were led off to the dungeon they lamented (to use a modern English version):

> O God, the heathen have come into thy inheritance;
>   they have defiled thy holy temple;
>   they have laid Jerusalem in ruins.
> They have given the bodies of thy servants
>   to the birds of the air for food,
>   the flesh of thy saints to the beasts of the earth.
>   (Ps. 79:1–2.)

The fourteen of them who were later led out to execution sang on from the same psalm until their tongues were cut out:

> Why should the nations say,
>   "Where is their God?"
> Let the avenging of the outpoured blood of
>   thy servants
>   be known among the
>   nations before our eyes!
> Let the groans of the prisoners come before thee;
>   according to thy great power preserve those
>   doomed to die!
>   (Ps. 79:10–11.)

When armed resistance began, Ps. 68 became the "Huguenot Marseillaise":

> Let God arise, let his enemies be scattered;
>   let those who hate him flee before him!
> As smoke is driven away, so drive them away;
>   as wax melts before fire,
>   let the wicked perish before God!
>   (Ps. 68:1–2.)

At the battle of Coutras, the Reformed soldiers knelt and prayed and sang. Roman Catholic courtiers, observing, cried out that they were afraid and were confessing, but a more experienced officer said it was not so. They were singing:

> This is the day which the LORD has made;
>   let us rejoice and be glad in it.
> Save us, we beseech thee, O LORD!
> O LORD, we beseech thee, give us success!
>   (Ps. 118:24–25.)

To know and love the psalms was the mark of a Protestant. The use of the psalter became a significant issue in the long nibbling away of the assurances of the Edict of Nantes. In 1623 singing of psalms was forbidden in streets and shops. In 1657 it was prohibited at executions; in 1658, anywhere outside "temples," as Protestant places of worship must be called. In 1659 psalms could not even be sung privately if audible outside, and in 1661 the singing of psalms anywhere in French territory became a felony.

So much for the psalms of the Calvinist service. There were, of course, sung prayers other than the psalms. The Song of Simeon was the hymn of thanksgiving after receiving the body and blood of Christ at the Communion. The Ten Commandments in French quatrains were also set to music, with the "Lord, have mercy upon us" (which was retained in Greek) as a prayer after each quatrain. Our

The Essentials of the Reformed Service

Lord's summary of the law is given a musical setting in some editions of the Huguenot psalter, and also the Lord's Prayer. And finally, one congregational act that was not Biblical in form, but wholly so in substance, was the singing of the Apostles' Creed. In the Middle Ages the Apostles' Creed was generally used only in Baptism and then in Latin. The Reformation saw a great expansion in its use, Calvin desiring it in every Lord's Day service in the vernacular as a congregational act. It was still continued in the baptismal service, of course, and used also in the weekday services and in family devotions and as a staple of religious education.

Such was the congregational sung liturgy in Calvin's service. The other prayers were spoken by the minister. Most of them were set prayers, although there was more freedom for variation than in any other major liturgical tradition of the time. But Calvin did not consider it wise to leave too much to the discretion of each individual minister. Let us see how it went together.

The minister opened the service, in the Strassburg tradition, with the solemn verse from the Mass:

> Our help is in the name of the LORD,
> who made heaven and earth. Amen.

The services of the Palatinate tradition preferred I Tim. 1:2:

> Grace, mercy, and peace, from God our Father, and Jesus Christ our Lord.

There followed at once the prayer of confession as a congregational act. This replaced the private confession of the priest before the Mass, for here was a congregational priesthood. The form of a general confession was probably derived from the medieval Communion orders and, like those, presupposed personal and specific confession outside the service. The general confession was to gather up and summarize the perpetual repentance of the whole people. They knelt at the pastor's call (with all Calvin's recognition of the necessary freedom and variety in such matters it was hard for him to conceive of any other posture in prayer). The words that Calvin adopted from Bucer were used thereafter in virtually every major Reformed order and even in a somewhat blander paraphrase, by Cranmer. They endure to this day in several, such as the Hungarian, the French, and the Scottish forms:

> Lord God, Almighty and everlasting Father, we acknowledge and unfeignedly confess, before thy Holy Majesty, that we are miserable sinners, conceived and born in corruption and iniquity, inclined to evil, unable by ourselves to do good, and that we continually transgress thy holy commandments, thus calling upon ourselves by thy just judgment, condemnation and ruin.
>
> Yet we are grieved, O Lord, because we have offended thee; we condemn ourselves and our sins in sincere repentance; we turn again to thy grace and implore thee to succor us in our distress. Have pity upon us, Gracious God, Father of mercies, and pardon our sins, in the name of Jesus Christ, thy Son, our Savior. Blot out our sins and stains and set us free. Multiply to us the daily mercies of thy Holy Spirit, that we may acknowledge from the heart and grieve at our unrighteousness, and beget a due repentance. Dying to all our sin, may we bring forth fruits of righteousness and purity which are well pleasing to thee, through Jesus Christ, our Lord. Amen.

Then in the Strassburg practice the minister read to the kneeling congregation some Scriptural promises of forgiveness, what Cranmer's book was to call the "comfortable words." Bucer used I Tim. 1:15; John 3:16 or 35 f.; Acts 10:43 or I John 2:1–2. (Cranmer was later to take over three of these.) The absolution followed:

Let each one of you acknowledge himself truly a sinner, humbling himself before God, and believe that the heavenly Father desires to be gracious to him in Jesus Christ;

To all who in this manner repent and seek Jesus Christ for their salvation, I declare absolution in the name of the Father, the Son, and the Holy Spirit. Amen.

When Calvin went back to Geneva, he found there some resistance to an absolution on the part of those who associated it with Roman abuses. "I yielded too easily"[19] he later confessed, and the Geneva congregation, by beginning to rise before the end of the confession, gave him no chance to repair the omission. But he left on record his judgment that an absolution should be included as at Strassburg.

In the Palatinate, Dutch, and Hungarian services the absolution, which was in the double form of a "binding" and a "loosing," came after the sermon instead of before. In all cases the Reformed services continued the medieval declarative form of absolution, rather than, as in the first millennium of the church, a prayer for forgiveness.[20]

The congregation rose to sing the Ten Commandments and the Kyries. In most Lutheran liturgies, and in the Reformed services of the Palatinate type, based on the preaching orders, the commandments were used *before* the confession as a guide for self-examination and accusation of conscience. Calvin rather used them *after* the absolution as a guide for the grateful obedience of the forgiven Christian, a use many Lutherans considered dangerously near to works righteousness. The Ten Commandments and Kyries were dropped, or at least made an alternative to a psalm, when Calvin returned to Geneva, but most Reformed liturgies used them, and they were restored in the French liturgy in 1639.

During the singing the minister left the table for the pulpit if he was not there already.[21] There he prepared for the reading and preaching of the Word by a prayer for the illumination of the Holy Spirit, that the Word might indeed cleave to the quick. This is one of the two prayers of the service which is free in Calvin's order, and even for this he provided some model prayers. The other prayer at the minister's discretion was the prayer after sermon, which in Calvin's custom was a bidding prayer, resuming the themes of the preached word in the form of petitions. In the orders of Palatinate type and the *Book of Common Prayer* there were no free prayers.

After the sermon and sermon prayer the minister returned to the table, in the Strassburg usage, and the people knelt for the great prayer of intercession: for those bearing political responsibility, for pastors and the church at large, for all men, and especially for those suffering affliction under war, disease, famine, poverty. This prayer at first concluded with a paraphrase of the Lord's Prayer, a medieval practice Calvin and Luther both adopted. From 1545 the Lord's Prayer itself was used instead, and in some Reformed churches it was sung by the congregation.

Then the congregation rose to sing the Apostles' Creed, while the minister prepared the bread and cup at the table for the third essential element of every assembly of the church. Or rather, such was Calvin's unfulfilled desire. From the beginning to the end of his ministry, at Strassburg and at Geneva, Calvin appealed to patristic practice and sought to join the Word preached and Holy Communion at every Lord's Day service. But in Strassburg he was able to effect this only monthly, and in Geneva it was at first observed only three times a year, then quarterly. Calvin reluctantly accepted what he considered a seriously defective custom, but he took care to put his vigorous protest on record in the hope of future amendment.[22] His order was always a truncated Eucharistic service, at the least. The Sacrament of the Table was the third element of every proper service of the church, along with the Word

The Essentials of the Reformed Service

read and preached, the prayers said and sung. In the Palatinate order the Lord's Supper was to be observed at least once a month in the towns, once every two months in the villages, in addition to Easter, Pentecost, and Christmas.

The variations in frequency of the Eucharist at first bore some relation to variant interpretations of its meaning. Zwingli, whose Eucharistic views Calvin found "almost profane,"[23] was quite content with a quarterly celebration. In Zwingli's service the predominant note is a joyful celebration of fellowship in the Christian body,[24] much in the spirit of the famous prayer of the Didache:

> As this broken bread was scattered over the mountains, and has been gathered together and made one, so may Thy Church be gathered from the ends of the earth into Thy kingdom.

In the early Basel service, on the other hand, one had, as it were, a Good Friday emphasis, in which "the whole matter is to meditate upon the passion of Christ."[25] With Bucer and Calvin, however, the most important meaning of the Sacrament is the mystical union of the faithful with the actually present risen Lord in his glorified humanity as something prior to and distinct from the appropriation of his gifts of forgiveness. This Calvinist emphasis on the actual presence, however, is present with the others in all the later national Reformed Communion services whether frequent or infrequent. The governing factors in the matter of frequency were evidently practical—the attitudes of magistrates, popular custom, and the availability of ministers.

The Calvinist stress on actual participation in Christ himself, "in such wise that He may live in us and we in Him," was the ground of the Reformed insistence on some form of closed Communion. This was the nerve of the concern for discipline in the church, that holy things be approached only in due reverence. Not that men could ever make themselves worthy to come into the presence of God. Quite the contrary, "we do not come to declare that we are perfect or righteous in ourselves, but ... by seeking our life in Christ, we confess that we are in death. ... All the worthiness which our Savior requires in us is to know ourselves, so as to be dissatisfied with our vices, and have all our pleasure, joy and contentment in him alone."

This requires that men be prepared for such a meeting. At Strassburg, as we have seen, Calvin required all who expected to take Communion to confer with the pastor beforehand. He wished to be sure that they understood the meaning of the Sacrament, to warn those living in open sin or hatred, to comfort those in anxiety with the assurance of God's promises. The so-called "fencing" of the Table, which was to become particularly associated with the Reformed tradition, was a common element in medieval Communion orders and not a Reformed invention. In Calvin's service it was located after the reading of the Scriptural warrant and promise from First Corinthians, when the pastor warned all those of scandalous life or without faith or understanding of the gospel not to come to the Table. The service had been announced the previous week, so that "each might prepare himself to receive it worthily and with becoming reverence." The listing of sins and crimes generally strikes the modern ear as unedifying and these portions of the liturgy, where, as in the *Book of Common Prayer,* they survive, are often nowadays omitted. But fencing was general pre-Reformation practice and reflects the situation of a state church where the total population was expected in church and wherein it was difficult to find a way for the exercise of discipline by the church apart from the magistrate.

The popular association of fencing with the Reformed tradition is just, however, for no other major Protestant tradition took the problem of discipline so seriously. Many

The Essentials of the Reformed Service

or most Reformed churches in Switzerland, France, Germany, the Netherlands, England, and Scotland passed through serious controversies over the control of the exercise of discipline, especially the ultimate sanction of excommunication. The frequency of celebration was affected, since it was usually connected with a disciplinary review of the whole congregation and thus made into an instrument of social control.

These struggles for social authority involved sociological tensions. The saying that Presbyterianism is no religion for a gentleman expresses the distaste of a privileged aristocracy for any review of its conduct. Such opinions were conspicuous among Dutch patricians, Anglican aristocrats, Huguenot nobility. The more popular classes in these countries were more inclined to support church discipline partly because it made for more social equality. These divergent pressures also affected issues of polity. In the nature of the case, synodical government gave more authority to the clergy and greater clerical independence of government. Kings and the aristocracy were best able to exercise control of church affairs through bishops. Congregationalism was calculated to give laymen on a local level a maximum of influence.

Those Reformed communities in which civil rulers won in these struggles, as in the Zurich or the Anglican churches, tended to minimize discipline. Clerical rigorism or even terrorism, on the other extreme, was the outcome for a time in Geneva, the Netherlands, Scotland, and New England. The reaction against such rigorism then often led to almost complete breakdown of any discipline. All this made for considerable diversity of practice in the several Reformed communities, but the exercise of public censure and excommunication and the procedure of restoration were familiar accompaniments of corporate worship in many Reformed communities.

The reading of the narrative of the institution of the

Holy Supper by Jesus as a warrant for the Sacrament was also a characteristic feature of the Reformed Eucharist. There one had at once the Lord's command to "do this" and his promise to make it fruitful.

The preliminary exhortation to Calvin's liturgy ended with an expansion of the ancient exchange, found as early as Hippolytus:

> Lift up your hearts.
> We lift them up unto the Lord.

The dialogue form as such survived only in the *Book of Common Prayer* among the services of the Reformed lineage, but the motif is developed more fully in the others. By itself the dialogue form of the "Lift up your hearts" does not necessarily convey its full original meanings. The author of the last book of Scripture reports how on the Lord's Day on Patmos he was caught up in the Spirit before the throne of God where worship is made perpetually. So, in the ancient church, the worshiping congregation understood itself as joined to that praise on high, the church militant and the church triumphant at one in adoration.

This wider dimension of the "communion of saints" was not adequately articulated in the Reformation liturgies. They did, however, stress communion in the Spirit with the ascended Christ as the aim of the "Lift up your hearts."[26] There was usually a polemic reference criticizing the focusing of devotion on the physical objects on the table, and then a summons to address ourselves to the reigning Lord of Life. "Let us raise our hearts and minds on high, where Jesus Christ is, in the glory of his Father, and from whence we look for him at our redemption.... Then only will our souls be disposed to be nourished and vivified with his substance, when they are thus raised above all terrestrial objects, and carried as high as heaven, to enter the Kingdom of God, where He dwells."

There is here a mixture of the metaphors of place and time to convey the reality of actual communion with God's presence from within a world as yet imperfectly redeemed, the already and the not yet. It is possible, these services affirm, to be actually united in the Spirit to the whole Christ who is yet to come, to participate in him even now as he dwells in the Kingdom and presence of God.

"This Kingdom," Calvin had explained, "is neither bounded by location in space nor circumscribed by any limits. Thus Christ is not prevented from exerting his power wherever he pleases, in heaven and on earth. He shows his presence in power and strength, is always among his own people, and breathes his life upon them, and lives in them, sustaining them, strengthening, quickening, keeping them unharmed, as if he were present in the body. In short, he feeds his people with his own body, the communion of which he bestows upon them by the power of his Spirit."[27]

In the ceremonial it was a characteristic of the Reformed services to stress the Table action, the actual breaking of the bread as symbolizing the sacrifice of Jesus' body. It was done solemnly in full view of the people, not buried away in a prayer and hidden by the body of the celebrant, as had come to be the medieval custom.

At the actual distribution the Reformed churches followed at least three distinct types of ceremonial. Calvin, and French and German Reformed, had the people come forward in line to receive standing at the table, as in the ancient church, usually the bread at one corner and the wine at the other. The Scots and Dutch preferred to serve the people seated at long tables in the nave. And the Zwinglians and Anglicans served the people in their places. In the forms of ceremonial in which it was necessary for the communicants to pass the bread and cup to each other there was usually conscious reference to the communion of saints. As Calvin had put it, "It is as if one said that the saints are gathered into the society of Christ on the principle that whatever benefits God confers upon them, they should in turn share with one another."[28] Calvin refused to make an issue of whether the bread and cup were to go from hand to hand, or to be served to each individually by a minister, or whether the wine be white or red (it never occurred to him that it might be unfermented) or the bread leavened or unleavened. Such matters were indifferent and left to the discretion of the church.[29]

Those who read later Pietism back into the sixteenth century and suppose the Reformers to have been preoccupied with an introverted and individualistic penitence should observe the substitution made at Strassburg for the "Lamb of God" of the Mass.[30] During the actual distribution of the elements the Strassburg congregation sang one of the triumph songs from the psalter, Ps. 138, read Christologically. A petition for individual forgiveness was replaced by the church's triumph in the accomplished victory of the Son. Each of the three stanzas of the French metrical version ends with:

Hallelujah! Hallelujah!

Then the minister gave thanks in language, originally from Bucer, which was to come down to us in both the Huguenot and Scottish services of Communion:

> Heavenly Father, we give thee undying praise and thanks for the great blessing which thou hast conferred upon us miserable sinners, in bringing us into communion with thy Son Jesus Christ, our Lord, whom thou didst suffer to be delivered to death for us, and now impartest to us as the food of everlasting life.
>
> Now, in continuance of thy goodness towards us, never allow us to become forgetful of these things, but grant rather, that carrying them about engraven on our hearts, we may grow and increase in a faith effectual to every good work. And so doing, may we dedicate the remain-

der of our life to the exaltation of thy glory and the edification of our neighbor,
through the same Jesus Christ thy Son, who lives and reigns with thee in the unity of the Holy Spirit, God forever. Amen.

The congregation rose from their knees to sing Simeon's song:

Lord, now lettest thou thy servant depart in peace . . . ;
For mine eyes have seen thy salvation . . .

and received the blessing of Aaron:

The LORD bless you and keep you;
The LORD make his face to shine upon you, and be gracious to you . . .

and were finally dismissed with a word about alms:

Remember Jesus Christ in his little ones.

This fourth and last necessary element in the service, the giving of alms, was thus appointed for the conclusion as the people left the service. There was no ceremonial presentation of offerings at an "altar"; the offertory of the Mass had shown the danger here. The meeting with Christ at the Table was to be continued in the world where he awaited discovery in the guise of the neighbor in need.

It must also be remembered that the Reformed service was the liturgy of a disciplined congregation and had necessary presuppositions of instruction, commitment, and weekday Christian obedience. The distinctive quality of Reformed worship was as much influenced by the character of the congregation as by the literary or musical vehicles of its praise. To abstract the prayers from this very specific social context and to study them in terms of literary quality or historical provenance misses precisely their liturgical meaning. To assess the Reformed services truly, one must consider the teaching, discipline, witness, and work of the congregation in relation to the worship.

III

THE MASS REFORMED

IT IS TIME TO TURN FROM GENERALIZED CHARACTERIZATION to the examination of specific orders of service. Most important and representative are the liturgies of the six chief national Reformed churches, the Huguenot, the Anglican, the Scottish, the Palatinate German, the Dutch, and the Hungarian, all but the last of which appeared within one generation. Certain other services of more local authority must also be noted, such as those of the Swiss cantons of Zurich, Basel, and Berne, and of à Lasco's refugee community in London.

These various regional orders of service may be grouped into two major types on the basis of their formal structure, although in the sixteenth century such a classification was viewed as much less significant than one by theological content and meaning. The two systems of organization do not coincide but cut across each other, a fact of considerable significance. The crucial theological divergencies concerned the manner of Christ's presence at the Eucharist and were crystallized from the Imperial Diet at Augsburg in 1530. The Lutherans affirmed a local presence "in" and "under" the bread and wine, while the Tetrapolitan Confession asserted a "true" presence in the sacramental action, but not localized in the physical objects (Zwingli also submitted a separate statement, but the major Reformed churches and even Zurich later adhered rather to the

The Mass Reformed

Tetrapolitan position). There were also important political animosities between the conservative imperialist Saxons and the republican and independent tendencies in the southern cities that precluded any genuine desire for theological understanding. Luther and Melanchthon went to Marburg determined to find *some* insuperable theological disagreement with the Swiss. They settled on the mode of the Eucharistic presence. If we refer to these two theological positions as "Lutheran" and "Reformed," we will find in each case two main types of formal liturgical structure.

The two liturgical patterns were both built on medieval models. One option was to translate and reform the Mass, whether a sung Mass or a "low" spoken Mass. The other was to take over two forms of services in the vernacular that had been developed in the Middle Ages, at least in southern Germany and Switzerland, the order for preaching services, and the order for administering Communion to the laity. The preaching service and the Communion service could be used either separately or in combination. Both of these two major options provided opportunities to restore the disrupted association of the congregational Eucharist and the preached Word, and, by means of vernacular psalms or hymns, to enable the laity once again to assume their proper role in the service. And this is what the leading Reformers attempted to do, by the one pattern or the other.

The option of utilizing medieval preaching and Communion orders was generally taken up in South Germany and Switzerland, in such Lutheran orders as those of Württemberg, Frankfurt, and Augsburg, and in such Reformed orders as those of Basel, Zurich, Berne, Schaffhausen, Montbéliard, Neuchâtel, and, at first, Geneva. Three of the later national Reformed liturgies, those of the German, Dutch, and Hungarian Reformed, also followed this pattern. We will consider this liturgical tradition in our next chapter. The present chapter will pursue the tradition based on the Mass, as illustrated in Luther's Wittenberg services, and in the Huguenot *Forme des Prières Ecclésiastiques,* the Anglican *Book of Common Prayer,* and the Scottish *Book of Common Order.*

As we turn to a consideration of the service books of the Reformation one general observation is in order. Contrary to notions sometimes held by later Puritans and Pietists, these books were not Roman Catholic in character, but a creation of the Reformation. They were not conceivable before the days of Gutenberg. The medieval missals had not been composed for the people, who could not have understood the Latin anyway, but for the clergy alone. But now all were to understand and participate in the service, which meant that, if possible, every literate layman should possess and use a service book. These same manuals would serve for private and family devotions as well as for Lord's Day worship, each enriching and deepening the other. The conception of a book of "common" prayer was a specifically Protestant idea.

We begin with the first Protestant services of Wittenberg and Strassburg, the mother cities of the Lutheran and Calvinist liturgical traditions respectively. Each proceeded by translating and editing the Mass, reintegrating the preached Word into the service, providing for Communion of the people, and rapidly preparing German language versions of psalms or hymns for the congregation.

Luther, the first and greatest sixteenth-century prophet of church reform, was curiously slow to turn his hand to matters of worship. He had more pressing matters to attend to, of course, and he had laid down the theological guidelines. But he allowed three or four other communities to precede him in the production of a German service, among them Strassburg. Not until 1525 did Luther's *Deutsche Messe* appear in print, and then only for the town of Wittenberg, as an example. Such was his reputation, of course, that his Wittenberg services were by far

The Mass Reformed

the most influential in all the northern part of the Empire. He began with the parish sung Mass, and retained the vestments, intoning, and altar ceremonial of the medieval service, although he conceded that "in the true Mass of real Christians the altar could not remain where it is and the priest would always face the people as doubtless Christ did at the Last Supper." He also retained the pericopes of the church year anthology, although he was not always happy about their selection.

In Strassburg, meanwhile, an Evangelical Mass had developed already.[31] The assistant at the cathedral, Diebold Schwarz, had produced a German Mass in 1524. It was built on a spoken "low" Mass, for the Evangelicals did not yet command the main parish service, but only a chapel. There was no choir accordingly, or intoning, and the ceremonial was much reduced. The "altar" became again a table, the "priest" a minister standing behind it, and ceremonial sprinklings, washings, genuflections, and elevations went out with the vestments. The Eucharistic prayer, however, was fuller than Luther's. A sermon and congregational singing were incorporated, the Strassburg psalter being a chief pioneer. As generally in South German Lutheranism also, the lectionary pericopes were shortly given up in favor of the patristic practice of continuous expository preaching. A series of sermons on, for example, John, Isaiah, Job, or Deuteronomy would be better able to set forth the Biblical message in its own proportions and movement, it was felt, than sermons based on someone's selections for an anthology. Such series would be interrupted, of course, for the half dozen major festivals of the church year. For a time there were two expositions in Strassburg; then, probably because of the problem of time, the readings and expositions were reduced to one, normally, on Sunday mornings, the Gospel.

The dominant figure in Strassburg from the middle 1520's was Martin Bucer, who was probably also the most important personal influence in the development of the Strassburg service in the next fifteen years until John Calvin arrived. We have already quoted two of his prayers that passed into the Reformed tradition as a whole, a confession and a post-Communion thanksgiving. In place of the medieval "gradual" between the readings Bucer often used a metrical version of the Ten Commandments, borrowed, probably, from the preaching order, as the exhortations before Communion probably came from the Communion order. While the metrical arrangements for congregational use were highly successful, several ancient elements that were not arranged for metrical congregational singing, such as the "Glory be to God on high," the "Lord, have mercy," the dialogue form of "Lift up your hearts," the "Holy, holy, holy" and "Blessed be he who comes," and the "Lamb of God," dropped out of use. It also proved difficult to persuade the people, accustomed to Communion only as a rare event, to come to the table every Lord's Day. But the outline of the Eucharistic order remained, even when it was reduced by lack of congregational participation to a "dry Mass." The minister conducted the service, with the exception of the reading and preaching of the Word, from the table.

Such, translated into French, was the basis of the liturgy of the Huguenot church. The earliest known French liturgy, to be sure, was Farel's *Manière et Fasson* of 1533 and the associated collection of musical arrangements. This had probably served Farel and his youthful assistant Calvin in their first, brief and stormy pastorate in Geneva. It was organized on the preaching and Communion orders. But neither Geneva nor the Reformed Church of France was to adopt this pattern of Lord's Day worship. The first full organization of the French Reformed was effected by John Calvin among the French exiles in Strassburg. There the enduring structure of Huguenot worship was established. The order is generally associated with Calvin's

The Mass Reformed

name, since it was disseminated by his influence, but he himself said that he borrowed most of it from the Strassburg German service.[32] Martin Bucer, consequently, as the leading Reformer of Strassburg, must be given credit as the chief architect of the Calvinist form of worship. It is worthy of note, perhaps, that Calvin used both patterns at different periods, the preaching order and Communion order combination and the Evangelical Mass, and preferred the latter.

The first collection of psalms (seventeen of them) were printed in 1539[33] and show Calvin's intentions. Back in Geneva, of course, Calvin and Farel had stipulated that the congregation should sing French versions of the psalms. In the ensuing year or so of controversy over discipline in Geneva, probably little was done to develop this suggestion. But in his relatively peaceful pastorate of the Strassburg refugee congregation Calvin evidently hunted about for metrical versions and somehow got hold of twelve as yet unpublished metrical translations by Marot, the first French poet of the day. Calvin himself wrote metrical French versions of five psalms (Ps. 25; 36; 46; 91; 138) and the Ten Commandments. The Strassburg tunes, already proved with the German psalms, were taken over. Apparently Calvin had his people singing from handwritten texts even before *Aulcunes Pseaulmes* appeared in print. Six months after he left in 1541 an edition of the psalms with the "Form of Prayers" was printed in 160 pages, the parent of the line of Reformed service books in French. In Geneva, also, the "Form" replaced Farel's service thereafter. We have today the Geneva edition of 1542 and the somewhat fuller Strassburg edition of 1545. There were lines of communication between the Strassburg church and some congregations in France, and the fuller Strassburg form was apparently used in some French churches, as at Meaux and Nîmes. But it was the shorter Geneva form which was generally adopted in France. There seems to have been no formal synodical adoption; the first reference we have is a stipulation of the Synod of Montauban[34] that it should not be changed. Strassburg, meanwhile, had fallen back into the hands of the Roman Catholics, and Bucer and Calvin's successor Pullain went into exile in England. Strassburg influence was to be felt there through Cranmer and in Geneva through Calvin, for Geneva succeeded Strassburg as the exile capital of French Protestantism.

After Calvin went back to Geneva, Marot soon appeared there also as a refugee. With Calvin's urging, Marot continued his translation and in 1543 published *Fifty Psalms*. The following year, however, he died in Turin, and the work waited until Beza arrived four years later. His versions began to appear in 1551 and at last the French psalter was complete in 1562. This psalter, with only slight revisions, has remained the liturgy of the French Reformed Church for the four hundred years since. As poetry it is far superior to the metrical versions in English, for here is an extraordinary variety of meters and rhyme schemes in contrast to the bald monotony of the English. Musically also, the work of Louis Bourgeois was rivaled by no later workman. There were one hundred twenty-five tunes, some in the medieval modal form, some in the modern major and minor. Douen estimates that about thirty of the tunes were borrowed from Strassburg and thirty-two more are recognizably related to current secular songs, often simply developments of an initial phrase. Bourgeois and Goudimel also arranged these melodies for choral singing in four to six parts, but Goudimel's preface (1565) is very explicit that these settings are not for church use but for singing in homes. Where harmonized settings became popular, however, they did tend to work their way back into church worship.

The Huguenots quite caught Calvin's concept of congregational psalmody. It became their hallmark, in homes, in corporate worship, or on the battlefield. The French

The Mass Reformed

Discipline required all to own and bring their liturgical psalters, and to share in the singing. The synods took the sung prayers very seriously. Figeac censured the practice of lining out (1579). Rochelle censured those who did not sing in service (1581). Synods of the early seventeenth century required the use of the whole psalm and ruled against the use of one or two stanzas only. They were not strictly held to psalms. Beza had introduced some hymns and these were authorized by the Synod of Montpellier (1598). However, in general little but psalms were sung in the sixteenth- and seventeenth-century French Reformed Church.

The twentieth-century Protestant Church locked six days a week has no precedents in the Reformation. All the Reformed churches of the sixteenth century conducted weekday services before and after working hours. We have noted the Geneva schedule. In Strassburg there was a weekday service of "morning prayer" with sermon in the parish churches at four or five o'clock in the morning. The service consisted of the general confession, the reading of Scripture and an exhortation based on it, a suitable pause for private prayers, closed by the minister with a collect and blessing. For late risers there was also a daily sermon at eight o'clock in the cathedral. The cathedral, again, was the scene for daily evening prayer with sermon. In this fashion provision was made for virtually everyone to attend worship with Biblical sermon twice daily either in the cathedral or in parish churches. Each series of services would follow its own systems of Bible readings, the Communion services on Sunday normally using the Gospels, the other services other portions of Scripture. One would expect also that the prayers of the weekday service would be more closely related to the particularities of lay vocations. A Lord's Day service which could presuppose such preparation would have a different character from the modern services which carry the whole week's burden of instruction and worship in one hour on Sunday morning.

From Strassburg, Calvin had carried the ideal of the disciplined church and the teaching of the "true presence" to Geneva and the Huguenot church. Bucer, meanwhile, was equally active in other directions. While Calvin was still at Strassburg, Bucer had been asked to draft an order of worship and discipline for Hesse (1539). This was the first church order with an independent church discipline, even to excommunication, and was thus a forerunner to Calvin's Geneva. Soon thereafter, when the Elector Archbishop of Cologne was preparing the reform of his electorate, Bucer was asked to draft his liturgy in collaboration with Melanchthon. The Cologne Reformation was suppressed by force when the Emperor finally opened war on the German Protestants. But Bucer's proposals for Cologne, and indeed Bucer himself, were to have more enduring consequences in England. To England we now turn for the second of our major Reformed liturgies.

The year 1547 was the one that shifted Reformed interest generally to England. Just as the Emperor won military control of Germany and forced many Protestant leaders into exile, the succession of Edward VI in England opened new prospects to the reforming movement there. Archbishop Cranmer was now able to formulate an evangelical liturgy and confession of faith for the English church. Indeed he hoped to unite the whole Protestant movement internationally by a council of representative theologians which could give a common answer to the papalists at Trent. Of all the leading Reformers, indeed, Cranmer, Bucer, and Calvin were those who labored hardest for the union of Protestantism. In this generation there was as yet little suspicion that episcopal orders or the lack of them might prove an issue in such an effort for union.

Of the Continental Reformers who now gathered in England, the largest group came from Strassburg, chief among them Bucer himself and Pullain, Calvin's successor as pastor of the French church. Bucer, together with

The Mass Reformed

three or four others, was given a theological chair. Pullain became pastor of a French congregation in Glastonbury. But the greatest concentration of refugees was in London. John à Lasco, onetime Polish baron, and more recently pastor at Emden, was made superintendent or bishop of the refugee church. The abandoned church of the Austin Friars was assigned to this "Church of the Strangers," and there services were held in French, Dutch, German, Italian, and other languages. The great majority of all the refugees were Reformed of one variety or another, rather than Lutheran. And the theological currents that influenced Cranmer's shaping of the liturgy and doctrine of the Church of England were overwhelmingly Reformed in character.

But Cranmer knew more of Lutheran worship than most Englishmen. He had been sent on an embassy to Charles V in 1531 and had observed developments in Nürnberg, the chief center of Lutheran liturgical influence in South Germany. Cranmer here had his first experience of the organization of Scripture readings on the basis of continuous reading rather than the church year, a pattern he was not to follow. But he did follow the Nürnberg feature of translating numbers of the collects from the missal into the vernacular. He became a friend of the Lutheran theologian Osiander and took back Osiander's niece to England as Mrs. Cranmer.

In the first year of Edward VI liturgical reform developed rapidly. Something was done for the incapacity of most English priests to preach with the publication of a book of homilies that summer. They might at least read someone else's sermons. And the following spring Cranmer had ready an English Communion order to be inserted in the Latin Mass after the Communion of the priest.[35] This was apparently the first vernacular order for lay Communion in England. In contrast to the Empire, no such service had developed before the Reformation in England.

Cranmer's consisted of an exhortation, words of invitation and of warning, a confession, absolution and "comfortable words," a prayer before reception, distribution, and benediction. The chief source was the Strassburg tradition, via Bucer's contributions to the Cologne liturgy. The confession in particular, with the promises of grace and the absolution, show substantial dependence, although for some reason Cranmer set the absolution *before* the "comfortable words" on which it was based.

Late in 1548 a commission of bishops and divines sat with Cranmer at Windsor and assisted him in the composition of a complete English language service book.[36] The Lord's Day service was built, like that of the Strassburg tradition, on the Mass, except that Cranmer's Mass was somewhat disorganized by its incorporation of his own originally independent Communion order. Thus the preparatory elements, like the confession and the absolution, which belonged at the beginning of the whole service in the Cologne order, occur in the middle of Cranmer's order, breaking it into two distinct services.

Unlike both the Strassburg and the Nürnberg orders, Cranmer's order retained the medieval lectionary and church calendar, with some reduction of saint's days. Cranmer supplied translated "collects" from the missal, as at Nürnberg, which were related, not always very obviously, to the Gospel or Epistle readings for the day. He composed relatively few new prayers, but displayed rare skill as an editor and translator, preserving in this way for the Church of England more of the utilizable literary heritage of medieval devotion than was secured for any other Reformed Church.

The *Book of Common Prayer* was also more akin to the North German type in its orientation to a sung mass rather than a spoken one. Prose psalms were retained by chanting, which presupposed the musical resources of a cathedral or city church rather than the average parish. Many

The Mass Reformed

traditional responses and hymns were retained in this way which had not been able to maintain themselves in the Strassburg tradition as merely spoken elements, such as the dialogue opening to the Eucharistic prayer beginning, "Lift up your hearts" and running through the "Holy, holy, holy." Cranmer seems to have made a conscious effort to preserve traditional forms and cadences while transforming meanings, as in his offertory prayer presenting a "sacrifice" of praise and dedication at the place where the Mass talks of a very different kind of "sacrifice."

While Cranmer repudiated any idea of priestly consecration or of a propitiatory sacrifice, he was scandalized to find that his Romanizing opponents could read these meanings back into his service by means of the ceremonial and ritual of the Mass, altars, vestments, lights, gestures. In the very year of its publication he began a revision of the Prayer Book to make its theology more explicit. The Council also ordered the bishops to remove altars from the churches and replace them by tables. Ridley and Latimer visited widely, clearing out images, shrines, and altars. And a violent controversy was occasioned by Hooper's intransigent refusal to wear the prescribed episcopal vestments.

In the preparation of revision Cranmer had at hand two other vehicles of Strassburg conceptions besides the *Consultation of Cologne*. In 1550 and 1551 Calvin's two services were published in England: the Geneva form, in English by Huycke; and the fuller Strassburg form, in Latin by Pullain. From the latter, Cranmer apparently borrowed the use of the Commandments combined with the "Lord, have mercy upon us, and incline our hearts to keep this law." The Geneva order, as we have seen, had dropped this use of the Commandments and Kyrie Eleison.

By 1552 the revised Prayer Book was ready. This was to be substantially the definitive Anglican liturgy, since Elizabeth's book of 1559 introduced few further modifications. In the revision of 1552 the most important single influence was the long *Censura* of Bucer, now professor at Cambridge.[37] On the whole, Bucer approved the 1549 orders for Communion and daily prayers. He disliked the prayer for consecration of the elements (epiclesis) which Cranmer had inserted in 1549 and this was removed as suggesting a local presence. But most of Bucer's criticisms related to rubrics and ceremonial. On the one hand, he opposed all the ceremonies that implied a propitiatory sacrifice or a spatial presence—vestments, altars, lights, chancels, elevation for adoration, genuflection, crossing, the placing of the bread in the mouth rather than in the hands. In fact the rubrics now moved from "altar" to "table" and specified that the table should be set out among the people, in the nave, or at the near end of the chancel. On the other hand, Bucer would have preferred a stronger affirmation of the true presence and more pressure for weekly Communion. Thus the formula for distribution to the people, "Take and eat this, in remembrance that Christ died for thee, and feed on him in thy heart by faith" seemed to be primarily shaped by à Lasco's memorialism: "Take, eat, and remember that the body of our Lord Jesus Christ was delivered to death. . . ." Interpreted in the light of the forty-two articles, however, of which Cranmer was also the chief architect, the somewhat Zwinglian tone of the Communion liturgy is corrected and the historian can agree with at least the nouns of the papal identification of Anglican worship with "the impious mysteries of Calvin." On the determinative issues of the Lord's Supper, the *Book of Common Prayer* finds its closest kin in Bucer and Calvin rather than in Lutheran or Roman services.

Controversy was precipitated by John Knox's sitting reception at Communion. This practice had been adopted by some English parishes since the 1549 book, following what they took to be the pattern of the Last Supper. So it

The Mass Reformed

was with Knox's Anglican congregation in Berwick and the Church of the Strangers in London. Those who advocated sitting regarded it as a retrograde step when the 1552 rubrics for the first time specified kneeling for the reception of the elements. Knox attacked kneeling in a sermon before the king as implying adoration of the elements. Cranmer held his ground, but an explanation was attached to the Communion liturgy denying explicitly any corporeal presence in the bread and wine. This "black rubric" was dropped in the Elizabethan book. A crossing of theological and ceremonial patterns is seen in the fact that while sitting Communion was originally associated with Zwingli, the Scots who adopted it following Knox were more emphatic on the true presence than the Anglicans who insisted on kneeling.

As was the case in Geneva the Strassburg ideal of a weekly service of Word and Sacrament was only imperfectly realized in England. The laity generally communed quarterly at most, although as in Geneva, the pattern of the Eucharist was before the people every week. The Anglicans were even less successful with the Word. A quarterly sermon was adequate in Queen Elizabeth's judgment, and two preachers to a diocese, and four out of five of her clergy were unable to preach. Most Anglican clergy were in fact lay readers who could not personally testify to the divine realities about which they read from printed homilies and prayers. The fact that 95 percent of them accepted every successive change under Henry, Edward, Mary, and Elizabeth of itself suggests that they possessed little religious comprehension. Calvin and Bucer both urged that preaching and teaching of the people were the most pressing reforms needed in England.

Cranmer's chief literary achievement was his arrangement of the Benedictine monastic services for daily prayers. The Spanish Franciscan Cardinal Quiñones had produced a reformed breviary, simpler and more Biblical, which Cranmer found to his use. He stitched together in this fashion the familiar services of morning and evening prayer of the Church of England. There had been numerous earlier attempts to consolidate the seven daily monastic services into two, one for morning and one for evening prayers. This brought weekday worship back to something like that of the fourth and fifth centuries, which was practicable for laymen. Luther devised such a scheme of morning and evening prayer in Saxony based on the monastic hours. Of all the similar sixteenth-century efforts Cranmer's alone has survived. In general, as we have seen, weekday services in the Reformed churches were less elaborate in pattern, usually including one psalm, a "chapter," and a prayer. The *Book of Common Prayer* services really presuppose a choir of monks or cathedral clergy; as has often been observed, the ordinary parish does not always find its needs well served by a service that requires so much liturgical and Biblical sophistication. As in the case of hymns, literary distinction may actually detract from liturgical value.

The "litany," which was Cranmer's first venture into English liturgy (1544), seems to have found no parallels elsewhere on the Reformed side unless one counts Bucer's contribution to the Cologne order, which Cranmer used. The litany consists of petitions and intercessions with congregational responses. It was to be performed after morning prayer three times a week. Both services make extensive use of brief spoken responses which place heavy demands on an unskilled congregation, and can seem artificial when recited back and forth by the clergy before a silent congregation.

For the people's liturgy the Church of England followed the Strassburg system of a metrical version of the psalms. Thomas Sternhold had begun the work with the publication of nineteen psalms in 1547. Two years later a posthumous edition of thirty-seven psalms appeared, which remained the English psalter for Edward's reign and most

The Mass Reformed

of Mary's. Hopkins added seven more in 1557 and the work was completed in 1562. The ballad meter was popular but monotonous in contrast to the Huguenot psalter.[38]

Most of Cranmer's work was in advance of the church generally. The first prayer book was unpopular in many or most parishes and various means were used to try to get people to attend public worship. The Prayer Book of 1552 and the following Articles of Religion never had time to prove themselves, for Mary and Philip of Spain carried through a Roman Catholic restoration in 1554. England, which had been a refuge for European Protestants since 1547, was now given over to a ferocious purge. Perhaps a fifth of the clergy were removed, mostly only for a few months, and scores went into exile, with larger numbers of laity, to Frankfurt, Zurich, Geneva. With them went back the earlier refugees from the Continent to England. Pullain took his French congregation to Frankfurt, where à Lasco also turned up after being denied asylum in Lutheran Scandinavia and North Germany.

From this movement of refugees was to come the service book of the third national Reformed Church. One hundred or more English refugees were received in Frankfurt, where they were permitted to share the use of the Church of the White Ladies with Pullain's French congregation, provided they would adopt the Strassburg confession of faith and ceremonies. This they were glad to do. But they had two liturgical options: an English translation of the Geneva order by Huycke and the Prayer Book of 1552. Parties formed, headed by Cox, once of the prayer book drafting committee, and Knox, who had, as we have seen, expressed some dissatisfaction with it already in England. Another English version of the Genevan type was drawn up early in 1555, probably chiefly by Whittingham, but it did not please the Cox party any more than Huycke's translation. Apparently one of the chief grievances with the Prayer Book, on the other side, was the use of spoken sentence responses in the various services, which were viewed by some as artificial and an impediment to reality in prayer. The Whittingham liturgy was also doctrinally more emphatic on original sin and grace and reflected more vividly the situation and mood of the persecuted exiles. Calvin was appealed to. It is not clear whether he was sent the Prayer Book or whether he knew it only from the description of its opponents. He observed that there were in it many inept things, which might still be tolerated, and he counseled reconciliation. But the Prayer Book Party forced Knox into banishment.

Knox went on to Geneva and there gathered another congregation of English refugees of about the same size as the Frankfurt group. They were assigned the use of the church called the "Auditoire" and adopted the liturgy rejected at Frankfurt, which was published in 1556 with a few metrical psalms. Thus originated the second chief Reformed liturgy in English. Knox took it back to Scotland in 1560, and in 1564, completed with additional prayers and a metrical psalter, it was adopted for the Church of Scotland. It was variously called the *Book of Common Order*, the *Form of Prayers, Knox' Liturgy, The Psalm Book*.[39]

In the Lord's Day service the order and some of the prayers were exactly those of Geneva. The intercessions, as one might expect, were different, although of the same character. In place of the single Scripture of Bucer and Calvin, however, Knox provided for two readings, one from the Old Testament and one from the New. In this way the relation of the two covenants would be kept before the people, something that might be lost with one reading only, or readings from Epistle and Gospel. As in Geneva and unlike Strassburg, the whole service was conducted from the pulpit. The constant reminder of the Lord's Supper which was conveyed by the Strassburg practice of leading the prayers from the table before and after sermon was thus lost from the weekly service. Again, while the Scots at first sought to celebrate the Sacrament

The Mass Reformed

monthly, in fact they were able to achieve the Genevan quarterly celebration only in the towns, whereas one annual Communion continued to be the custom in the country parishes. A major factor in this breakdown of the balance of Word and Sacrament was the desperate shortage of ordained ministers. In 1567 there were only 289 ordained men in Scotland, and two thirds of the parishes must needs be served by unordained "readers" who were not qualified to administer the Lord's Supper.

The sung prayers were built on the core of Sternhold's and Hopkins' metrical psalms. In Geneva the attempts to translate the remaining psalms into the elaborate meters suited to the French musical settings were rarely successful. The great bulk of the psalms were done in common meter, consequently, and the number of utilizable tunes was thus greatly reduced. The Scots psalter, however, did acquire about twice as many tunes as the English and thus permitted more metrical variety also. It was to become also more deeply embedded in the affection of the church, and the spoken liturgy less so, than in Anglicanism.

In some editions of the Huguenot, Dutch, and Scottish psalters are found a full set of 150 collects, one for each psalm. Since the psalms were scheduled systematically, this yielded, in effect, another type of "collect for the day." Thus, for example, upon Psalm 69 was set forth the following (in the Scots dialect):

> Eternal Father, and God of all consolatioun, that for the satisfactioun of our sinnes, wald cast down thy onelie Sonne to extreame dolours and anguishes, and hes ordayned thy Kirk to pas be the samin way of affliction:
>
> We beseik the maist effecteouslie, that forsamekill as we are destitute of all help of men, we may sa mekill the mair be assurit of thy mercie and gudenes, that we may praise the sam before all creatures, baith now and euer mair. So be it.

In the ceremonial of the Lord's Supper the Scots diverged from the French and the English Reformed. Instead of bringing the people forward to receive standing or kneeling about the table, Knox, as we have seen, had early preferred à Lasco's custom of seating communicants at a long table in close imitation of the Last Supper. This meant that special tables were set up in the church at Communion time, and that on other Lord's Days there was no table in evidence at all.

Weekdays prayers were conducted in the town churches by lay readers. As in Lutheran Germany the schoolmaster carried this burden more often than the pastor. The Scriptures were to be read through systematically, Old Testament and New, and the reader led in the singing of a psalm.[40] Sometimes also the Creed, the Commandments, the Lord's Prayer, or the prayer of confession were used. There were musical settings in the Psalm Book for the Lord's Prayer and Commandments. In the majority of sixteenth-century parishes the Lord's Day services were also conducted by the readers, following the *Book of Common Order*. In those parishes where there was an ordained minister the reader's service came first, and the minister (with some of the congregation) entered only just before the sermon. The minister also felt freer to substitute prayers of his own for those of the stated liturgy. A similar institution developed in Continental Reformed churches toward the end of the century, the French with their *lecteurs* and the Dutch with *voorlesers*. Without it the daily services would hardly have been possible.

In each of the three classical liturgies of the French, English, and Scottish Reformed churches we have seen variants on the structure of the Mass with preached Word. Theologically the crucial definition was the "true presence" in the Eucharist. We must now turn to another family of Reformed liturgies holding the same doctrine, but related structurally to medieval preaching and Communion services.

IV
PREACHING AND COMMUNION ORDERS REFORMED

IN THE NORTHERN AND RURAL PARTS OF THE EMPIRE THE evangelical communities organized their worship after Luther's example, on a reform of the Mass. The more common pattern, on the other hand, in the towns of South Germany and Switzerland (with important exceptions we have already considered) was a combination of the two vernacular services already familiar there, the preaching order and the order for lay Communion. The difference seems to have been regional and cultural rather than theological; Lutheran and Reformed alike are found using both patterns.

For an illustration of a later medieval preaching order in the vernacular we may take the one in which Zwingli began his ministry, that of the Basel professor and pastor Johan Surgant.[41] Zwingli made a minor change or two in the sequence, which was variable anyway, but took over the form entire. It began with a prayer for illumination in the hearing of the Word, proceeded to the intercessions, the Lord's Prayer, the "Hail Mary" (Zwingli also defended her immaculacy in *Of Mary the pure mother of God*), then set the Scripture and the sermon. Then followed a list of those who had died during the week (these were plague times) and a prayer of thanks for them, the Ten Commandments, general confession, and prayer for forgiveness. The Lord's Prayer, the "Hail Mary," and the Creed sometimes preceded and sometimes followed the sermon. But the location of the Commandments, the confession and absolution after the sermon seems to have been a matter of principle, since the sermon was conceived as directed to repentance. So Zwingli preached as a Roman priest and so he preached grace from 1519. He did make a new emphasis by preaching "in course" a series of expository sermons on Matthew. He was to preach daily for a dozen years, and in the course of it, to change the face of Zurich permanently. Around this service an evangelical community was gathered before the public Mass was reformed. The preaching service by that time was established as the normal and sufficient Lord's Day service.

Zwingli's preaching order appears with but slight variations also in Berne (*Agendbuchly*, 1529) and Schaffhausen, and in French in Farel's *Manière et Fasson* (1533),[42] which was used in Geneva for a time, in Neuchâtel, and in Montbéliard. For our purposes it is not necessary to attempt to resolve the question whether the Berne order was based on Farel's early Montbéliard draft of 1524 or 1525, or whether, contrariwise, the *Manière et Fasson* was a French version of the *Agendbuchly*. That a family relation exists is sufficient for us. The sequence in the *Manière et Fasson* begins with a prayer for the Holy Spirit and the intercessions for magistrates and the congregation, ending with the Lord's Prayer. Then comes the Scripture and its exposition "word by word without leaving the text," then the Decalogue and the general confession, the Lord's Prayer again, the Apostles' Creed, a final prayer of intercessions for those ignorant of God's truth, for the bereaved, for the persecuted, for grace to use the sword rightly, and last, the blessing. The general similarity to Zwingli's order is apparent, with all the variations.

Farel was also, we may note parenthetically, the chief agent in establishing the close association of the Italian Waldensians with the Reformed churches. This pre-Reformation community in their mountain valleys had heard of the Reformation. They sent a deputation to Luther in 1526 without result. Four years later the Synod of Mérindol commissioned representatives to visit the Swiss Reformers, and invited a return visit. Farel attended the two-week synod in 1532 and made such a strong impression that the synod voted to join the Reformation movement. Thenceforth the *"barbes"* were often trained at Geneva or Lausanne. This probably involved a gradual transition from the previous Biblical legalism and discipleship of the Waldensians, akin to that of the Anabaptists, to justification by grace. In worship the simple prayer, Scripture, and exhortation of the Waldensians was very close to the Farel type of preaching order already. As we shall see later, the other pre-Reformation "Protestant" community, the Bohemian Brethren, was also to establish close ties with the Reformed.

For the medieval vernacular Communion orders we lack such a pat instance as Surgant provides for the preaching service. The known texts must be dated after the beginning of the Reformation.[43] But of the existence of pre-Reformation orders there can be no doubt. They usually contained exhortations on the proper approach to the Sacrament, "fencing" off of the scandalous and ignorant, public confession and absolution. Farel's *Manière et Fasson* presents such a Communion order, featuring a reading of the narrative of the institution as a warrant and a summons to the faithful to raise their hearts to the presence of the risen Christ.

Such orders were combined with preaching orders to give the most widespread pattern in South German Protestantism. Perhaps the earliest such service on the Reformed side was that of Basel, the so-called *Form und gstalt* (1525 or 1526),[44] which was practically contemporaneous with the Strassburg and Wittenberg services. The combination of the preaching and Communion services was a frequent one, since Communion was scheduled every Sunday in one of the city churches and every month or so in the Basel countryside. The Lutheran order of Württemberg (1536) was similar in structure, but Communion was less frequent. On both the Lutheran and Reformed side services of this type were performed without the paraphernalia and ceremonial of the Mass, and the church year pericopes were replaced by systematic preaching in course.

Zurich provides a rather exceptional development in Eucharistic liturgy as well as doctrine. Zwingli did not, like Oecolampadius at Basel, adapt an existing Communion order. When he finally attempted a Protestant Communion at Easter of 1525, it was something original, one of the few new liturgical creations of the Reformation.[45] It was conceived as an occasional service and scheduled for Christmas, Easter, Pentecost, and once in the autumn. He utilized several elements from Low Mass, such as the Introit, "Glory be to God on high," and the Creed, which he wished recited responsively by the congregation, since all music was excluded. He also kept the vestments and the assisting deacon. His ceremonial was probably influenced by the Anabaptists Grebel and Hubmaier, who had conducted a Communion the preceding year in Zurich with the communicants seated around a table as at the Last Supper. Zwingli had the table set out in the nave and gathered the people about it. The minister and deacon served them there in their places, instead of having them come up in line as was usually done, and as was done, in fact, in Zurich canton outside the city. This method of serving was later to be adopted by Elizabethan Anglicans.

These merely local Swiss services built of preaching and Communion orders were succeeded in the second half of the century by another generation of Reformed liturgies on the same scheme, but for national churches. These are the services we have referred to as those of the Palatinate tradition, the Palatinate German liturgy, the Dutch liturgy, and the Hungarian. But while in structure they are closer to the liturgies of Basel and Zurich than to those of Strassburg or Scotland, the doctrine is similar to that of the services of Mass type. Mere "memorialism" had been laid aside even in Zurich since 1549.

The pioneer of this second family of services was the Polish nobleman John à Lasco. He had been an Erasmian Catholic, but in 1538 declined a bishopric and joined the Reformed Church, serving as a pastor at Emden, on the Dutch border of western Germany, under Archbishop Hermann of Wied. Emden was a refuge for Dutch fugitives from the Spanish Inquisition in the Low Countries, and such were the bulk of à Lasco's parishioners.

After the defeat of the Protestants by Charles V and the imposition of the "Interim," as we have already seen, à Lasco, with numerous other Continental Reformers, took refuge under the hospitable regime of Edward VI in England. He lived with Cranmer over the winter of 1548/49 and in the following years was with Hooper the most vigorous champion of the "Zwinglian" party in England. He also exercised a kind of episcopacy over the refugee congregations and their ministers who were given the use of the Church of the Austin Friars in London.

À Lasco drew up a full plan of government and discipline, as well as worship, for the Church of the Strangers, which was organized in 1550. Whether the *Forma ac Ratio* was actually completed that year we do not know, since it remained in manuscript throughout the life-span of the refugee congregation. In 1553, upon the accession of Mary, the exiles were cast loose again to wander on the Continent. The order was first printed in a Dutch abridgment by Utenhove at Emden in 1554, and in entirety in Latin in 1555 in Frankfurt.[46] The short Dutch version was used by the Emden congregation for some years. The longer version was to shape the definitive Dutch liturgy by a more circuitous route.

The Lord's Day order for the *Forma ac Ratio* was a typical preaching order. All proceeded from the pulpit, in contrast to the Strassburg and Anglican Mass orders. There was an opening summons to worship, then a prayer for illumination before sermon, ending with the Lord's Prayer. One of the two psalms of the service was inserted at this point, a practice then still unknown at Zurich. Then the preacher read his Scripture and preached, it was recommended, not more than an hour. There was but one lesson, as with Bucer and Calvin, and these were to be taken in continuity from "some Biblical book of the Old or New Testament." The sermon was to be faithful and complete exposition, not philosophy or human traditions or histories, or small selected scraps of Scripture "as is ordinarily done in popery." The sermon was followed by a prayer for the fruitfulness of the Word.

The various elements after the sermon, as was usual in preaching orders, offered several options. The Ten Commandments, if used, came before the general confession and absolution, as had been done by Farel, whereas Calvin, as we have seen, reversed the order. À Lasco's form of absolution was a double one, of binding as well as loosing, and thus especially solemn. Then might follow the Creed and general intercessions, for magistrates, ministers, brothers under persecution, those in Roman ignorance and idolatry, for the church of refugees, ending with the Lord's Prayer for a second time.

After the intercessions and supplications, marriages or baptisms were celebrated as occasion arose, congregational announcements were made, and every month the Communion order was used. The service ended with a second psalm, the blessing, and a summons to remember the poor.

Three features in particular of the *Forma ac Ratio* were to have a history in successor services, the catechetical service, the service of preparation for Communion, and the Communion ceremonial.

Preaching and Communion Orders Reformed 77

The service after noon on the Lord's Day, first of all, featured a systematic exposition of the catechism, for which room was made by a shortening of the sermon. The Commandments, confession and absolution, and Creed were also omitted. In this way a regular program of theological instruction was built into the weekly schedule.

The monthly Communion service, in the second place, was to be announced two weeks in advance. The prospective communicants were to be reviewed by the elders. And then on the Saturday before, a special service of preparation was to be held, with an exhortation, a psalm, and a blessing. Such a preparation of itself suggests that the Eucharist to follow signified more than merely a memorial.

The Communion service, finally, followed the dramatic ceremonial of actually seating the communicants at a long table, the presiding minister in the center facing the congregation. There before the watching church he broke the bread and ate and served those on either side, the plates moving out to the ends of the table, each taking a piece. So it went likewise with the cup until all were served. Then the communicants rose and left and the places at the table were again filled as the rest of the congregation came forward in two lines from each side. When the table was again ready the minister again broke bread and served the cup for the second sitting, and so with the third, and as many as were needed. A reader, meanwhile, read the sixth chapter of John during the intervals, and if there was time, also the thirteenth, fourteenth, and fifteenth chapters, and others if necessary. Such was the ceremonial, as we have seen, which Knox preferred to the kneeling reception of the 1552 *Book of Common Prayer*. Anglicans, on the whole, were not to adopt it, but it was to be used by the Dutch and Scots for generations.

A chief legatee of this service of the Church of the Strangers was to be the fourth of our national Reformed orders, the German service book of the Electorate of the

Palatinate.[47] Protestantism had reached the Palatinate in 1545, later than any other major portion of the Empire. The religious situation was still fluid at the end of the 1550's when Frederick the Pious became Count. There were at least four contending parties, the strict Lutherans, the followers of Melanchthon, Calvinists, and Zwinglians. Frederick steered his way through the debates, adopting the middle ground of Calvin and Melanchthon. He set Ursinus and Olevianus to draft a new confession, and with Tremellius, to draw up a liturgy. The results were the Heidelberg Catechism, the best of the Reformed catechisms, and the Palatinate Church Order, both ready in 1563.

The Palatinate services owed most to the *Forma ac Ratio*, especially for the Lord's Day. The Lutheran order which they replaced, to be sure, was also a preaching order, so there was no fundamental change in structure. After the opening salutation, "Grace, mercy, and peace . . . ," the bulk of the prayer before sermon was the Bucer-Calvin confession, to which was added a short prayer for illumination and the Lord's Prayer. The preaching was to be expository, in course, and preachers were to attend to the threefold pattern of leading men first to knowledge of their sin, then of their redemption, and finally how they should show their thankfulness. After the sermon came the Württemberg (Lutheran) form of confession, and after the Scriptural promise of redemption, the solemn double proclamation of forgiveness and of judgment, modeled on that of the *Forma ac Ratio*.

> Now, as many as there be of you, who despair of themselves and their sins, and trust that their debts are completely forgiven to them through the merit of Christ alone, who resolve more and more to desist from sins, and to serve the Lord in true holiness and righteousness:
> To those (as they believe in the Son of the living God) I proclaim at God's command that they are released in

heaven from all their sins (as He doth promise in His holy Gospel) through the perfect satisfaction of the most holy passion and death of our Lord Jesus Christ. Amen.

But as many as there be among you, who still take pleasure in their sins and shame, or persist in sins against their conscience:

To such I declare by the command of God that His wrath and judgment abideth upon them, all their sins being retained in heaven: And they can never be delivered from eternal damnation, except they repent.

After the sermon came the thanksgiving and intercessions—for the Emperor, princes, lords, especially Count Frederick, his wife and children, and the city council of Heidelberg, for the poor, those suffering persecution from the Turk or the pope, for widows, orphans—concluding with the Lord's Prayer. An alternative here was an extended paraphrase of the Lord's Prayer, a form also used by both Luther and Calvin. Then came the one psalm of the service and Aaron's blessing.

On Sunday afternoons the commandments and the Creed were included and the service found its focus in a sermon on the appointed questions from the Heidelberg Catechism, which was broken up into units for each Sunday of the year. A Lasco's catechetical service was thus consolidated. The result had some of the utility of a church year lectionary, in that the full cycle of Christian affirmations was set before preacher and congregation systematically each year. The main holy days were also observed, Easter, Ascension, Pentecost, Christmas, and also New Year's Day, but otherwise the morning readings and sermons were "in course."

Morning and evening prayers were also supplied for weekday services. There was always a chapter with a brief exposition and the Lord's Prayer. The Ten Commandments came in the morning and the Creed in the evening service. On Wednesdays and Fridays psalms were sung before and after the sermon; other weekday services did not have singing. From 1573 the most popular German psalter was Lobwasser's translation of the Huguenot book, and the Palatinate prayers usually appeared in its back pages. Other Reformed regions of Germany used the Palatinate church order also. The liturgy of the Synod of Jülich, Cleves, Berg, and Mark, for example, was a variant.

The Lord's Supper was to be celebrated at least once a month. Notice was to be given the week before and on the day before, as in the *Forma ac Ratio,* a preparatory service was to be held. A sermon was to be preached on the true understanding of the Sacrament, new candidates for admission to the Supper were to be examined before the congregation, and then the whole congregation was charged in public question and answer to confess their sin, affirm their faith, and dedicate themselves in thankful devotion. This series of formal questions and answers was a new pattern, but it has maintained itself in some quarters, as in the Hungarian church, to this day.

The Lord's Supper was celebrated the following morning after the sermon and intercessions. It began with the narrative of the institution, exhortation to self-examination, fencing off of various categories of sinners and a reminder, in Calvin's language, that contrition, not sinlessness, is the qualification for admission. Then came a thankful memorial for the full work of redemption by the incarnation, life and passion of Jesus, the institution of the Supper as a seal of the new covenant, and the work of the Holy Spirit in bringing us into true communion with Christ and one body through brotherly love, "as of many grains, one flour is ground and one bread is baked."

An invocation of the Holy Spirit then followed that "our . . . hearts may be fed and quickened by His true body and blood" so that we may "in all tribulations wait with head uplifted for our Lord Jesus Christ out of heaven, when He will make our mortal bodies like unto

His transfigured and glorious body and take us to Himself in eternity." Similarly, after the Creed, we are enjoined to "lift up our hearts and faith unto heaven, where Christ Jesus is our Intercessor . . . and doubt not that through the action of the Holy Spirit, our souls shall be fed and nourished with His body and blood, as truly as we receive the holy bread and cup in remembrance of Him." Communicants came forward and received standing rather than adopting à Lasco's sitting Communion.

Our fifth national Reformed church, that of the Dutch, was to align itself with the Palatinate pattern of worship. Services had been conducted in Dutch, as we have remarked, in the London refugee congregation of à Lasco in the days of Edward VI. But whatever order was used, whether that printed in Emden in 1554 by Utenhove, or a Dutch translation of the *Forma ac Ratio*, or something else, it was not destined to become the authorized order of the Dutch Reformed. When the first general synod (1568) of the Dutch Reformed Church met in exile at Wesel, a Lutheran city on the lower Rhine, they adopted *De CL Psalmen* of Peter Dathenus, with its attached prayers, as their official liturgy. The psalter, as the title states, was a translation of the Huguenot psalter, already in use among the Walloons. And the minister's prayers were a Dutch adaptation of those of the Palatinate liturgy, done by Dathenus as pastor of the Dutch refugees at Worms in the Palatinate in the early 1560's. He also translated the Heidelberg Catechism for his people.

During the troubled decades of the Dutch war for independence the Reformed order manifested some variations, often apparently influenced by the Calvinist service as available to the Walloons. Thus the opening "Our help is in the name of the Lord" was sometimes preferred to the Palatinate "Grace, mercy, and peace." And there was variation in the location of the Creed, the Ten Commandments, and the use of an absolution. Some congregations used the medieval pericopes for a time, but the synods preferred continuous exposition of whole books of Scripture. The final stabilization of the "Netherlands Liturgy" did not come until the Synod of Dort in 1619. There the Commandments were assigned to the morning service on the Lord's Day and the Creed to the catechetical service in the afternoon. A form for adult baptism was added, probably for the missions in Indonesia and New Amsterdam. It is interesting to observe that within a decade of the landing of the Pilgrim Fathers, both the Dutch and the Huguenot Reformed liturgies were in use on Manhattan island. In the ceremonial of the Supper, the Dutch adopted à Lasco's sitting at long tables, in contrast to the Palatinate standing reception. The text of the service is very close to that of the Palatinate, blending Zwinglian and Calvinist themes.

From these German and Dutch church orders we now turn to a last group of Reformed churches, those of eastern Europe. East of Germany the Reformed tradition gave early promise of strong churches in Poland, Bohemia, Lithuania, Hungary, Transylvania. This was mostly feudal territory, with little political organization or urban life. Bohemia, the home of the Hussite rising of the fifteenth century, was the most developed of these countries. Hungary and Transylvania were largely in the control of the Moslem Turkish invaders. Poland and Lithuania comprised a mighty sweep in the sixteenth century, from the Baltic to the Black Sea, from the Ukraine to Danzig, marking the frontier of Western Christendom with Orthodox Muscovy. The populations were Slav or Magyar generally, but colonies of Germans and Jews were scattered about, constituting the chief commercial class in these countries. In all of them, Reformed ideas and communities spread rapidly in the second half of the sixteenth century, finding a readier response among Slavs and Magyars than did Lutheranism, which was successful rather among the Germans.

Preaching and Communion Orders Reformed

In Bohemia and Poland the Hussite church, the Bohemian Brethren, established close relations with the new Calvinist movement, and with the more ecumenical wing of the Lutherans. The Polish Calvinists united with the exiled Bohemian Brethren in 1555 at the Synod of Kózminek, adopting the Bohemian liturgy, confession, and episcopacy. À Lasco arrived the next year as an exile from Mary and labored for the next four years until his death as a bishop or superintendent of this Reformed-Bohemian church. Calvin, who, for whatever reasons, had recommended episcopal organization to the king of Poland, thoroughly approved the merger and urged union also with the Melanchthonian Lutherans. A federal union with intercommunion with these Lutherans was achieved by the Consensus of Sendomir in 1570. In similar fashion the Lutherans, Calvinists, Bohemian Brethren, and Utraquists of Bohemia drafted a joint "Bohemian Confession" five years later. Both agreements took the common Eucharistic position of Melanchthon and Calvin, which was repudiated by the more exclusive Lutherans.

In both Poland and Bohemia, however, the Counter-Reformation of the following decades gained back most of the Protestant territory. In Bohemia the scorched-earth policy reduced the population from four millions to eight hundred thousand and nearly wiped out Czech literature and culture. No influential liturgical tradition survived these persecutions. The life of these stillborn churches, however, shows the adaptability and variety of Reformed worship within the necessary agreement on theological fundamentals.

In Hungary and Transylvania, on the other hand, the Reformed Church of the Magyars was to survive atrocious oppression to become the largest Reformed church on the Continent. The story of Hungarian Protestantism is a complicated one on which there is little information in Western languages, but a few generalizations may be hesitatingly ventured. The region was dominated by the Turks in the period of the first penetration of Protestant ideas, and the political situation varied in the different regions. After the disaster of Mohács (1526) the Turks occupied the strategic center; the Catholic Hapsburgs were strongest in the West; and the Magyar area of the East lived in a status of dependency. The first Protestant propaganda was chiefly Lutheran, especially from Wittenberg, but Reformed influence was also felt in the 1540's. By the mid-century, Protestantism generally was stronger than Roman Catholicism and in the second half of the century the various tendencies, Lutheran, Reformed, and later, Unitarian, increasingly consolidated as separate churches. In the western area there was a consistent effort to maintain effective cooperation of Lutherans and Reformed until deep into the seventeenth century. But in eastern Hungary a distinctively Reformed church life defined itself. These diverse tendencies were reflected in the history of Protestant worship.

In the West there was a series of liturgical publications of a prevailingly North German Lutheran type. Various collections of Hungarian hymns appeared from the 1530's, books carried and sold by itinerant preachers. The work of Gáspár Heltai (1550) is characteristically Lutheran. Gál Huszár wrote Bullinger for advice about fifteen years later, but when he published a liturgy in 1574 it was apparently modeled not on Zurich practice but on Luther's *Formula Missae,* a sung Mass, with some portions still in Latin. According to Huszár's letter there was at that time no unified pattern among those who considered themselves Reformed. A similar effort, following the Wittenberg type, appeared as late as 1636 with the order of János Samarjai. Various antiphons and responses were widely used.

The definitely Reformed type of worship and theology grew up in these same years in eastern Hungary. Péter Méliusz Juhász, bishop of Debrecen, was the chief agent in the process. He was a leader in the drafting of the Reformed Confession of Debrecen in 1562 and at the Council of Debrecen of 1567 which clarified the organization of the Reformed churches as well as adopting the second Helvetic Confession and the Heidelberg Catechism. There were then two dioceses, the one of the Tibiscan Valley centered at Debrecen, the other in Transylvania with Francis Dávid as bishop. Later three more dioceses were to be organized. Church government was controlled by bishops, deans, pastors, and lay magnates, with little congregational voice in affairs. The Palatinate liturgy was translated into Hungarian by the younger Huszár in 1577, and from that time was to gain influence as the normative Reformed pattern of worship.

The increasing solidity of this definitely Reformed church is reflected in the bitter hostility of the Lutheran Keresztur Ágenda of 1598, which opens with a prayer that the Calvinists should be either converted or destroyed.

After Méliusz the most important figure in the definition of Hungarian Reformed worship was Albert Szenci Molnár. Molnár composed what was to become the definitive Hungarian metrical psalter, using Lobwasser and the Huguenot psalter as well as the original Hebrew, and writing in what is described as beautiful Hungarian verse. This version evidently won out in time over the *Debrecen Psalter* (1592) of Bishop György Gönczi, although the latter saw fourteen editions in the seventeenth century. But Molnár accompanied his *Hungarian Psalter* of 1607 with translations of the Palatinate liturgy. Amid the ecclesiastical and political disorganization of the country there was no body that could adopt a liturgy for the whole national church. Perhaps Molnár's publication of 1607 is the nearest we can come to a representative service book. A dozen or so years later István Milotai Nyilas published another liturgical work, also based on the Palatinate liturgy, which was to be influential through the seventeenth and eighteenth centuries.

Two or three general observations may be made by way

of a conclusion to this historical analysis of liturgical structures. It would be neater if the two main patterns could be identified with the Lutheran and Reformed traditions in principle, and this has often been done. But in fact the governing factors seem to have been cultural and sociological differences and matters of sheer historical contingency, such as the opportunities open to reformers in the various communities. And there are too many exceptions to justify the correlation with doctrine. What more loyal Lutheran could one find than the Württemberger Brenz? And what more representative Reformed churchman than Calvin? Each must be treated as an exception if one attempts to define a confessional liturgical type. And if one views Elizabethan Anglicanism as Reformed, as was generally done on doctrinal grounds in the sixteenth century, one has a Reformed church with the medieval pericope system and, at least around the court, although not generally, the full paraphernalia of an "altar" service. It would seem to be nearer the truth and closer to the sixteenth-century view to consider liturgical structure within the recognized theological guidelines as an optional matter, in which there is neither a Lutheran nor a Reformed "type."

A further observation is that the classification of structures into those of Mass type and those of preaching and Communion orders becomes less significant in practice, since the two tend to converge. The Mass originally developed in the second century, after all, out of the combination of a preaching order and a Communion order. And a spare service of Mass structure but without Communion does not differ greatly from a preaching order. There was not, after all, so great a difference between, say, the worship of the Church of Scotland at the end of the sixteenth century and that of the Reformed Dutch across the North Sea, although the two services had grown up in rather different ways.

To turn from structure to tone, certain other reflections come to mind as we look back over the formation of these half dozen Reformed liturgies, of the French, English, Scottish, German, Dutch, and Hungarian churches. When we read them today one of the most striking characteristics is the pervasive sense of persecution and danger. Unlike the Lutheran orders, which were generally composed and put forth under public authority, the Reformed services are more characteristically the work of churches organized in defiance of the government. A liturgy like Cranmer's, composed in an archbishop's palace, is exceptional among them. Most of these orders of service were written by exiles in refugee communities, in Strassburg, Geneva, Frankfurt, London, Emden, Frankenthal. They use naturally the appeals of the psalmist for deliverance from enemies seeking a very literal destruction. They voice the praise of men who have paid a great price in blood and treasure, who hope, against all prudential calculation, in the Lord. As a group these are the liturgies of the churches under the cross, or under the "Holy Office." Practically every family in Calvin's Geneva had lost a member or a close friend. Among them were fifteen hundred French families, three hundred from Italy, others from England, Scotland, Germany, the Netherlands, Poland, Hungary. In the Netherlands alone, as Gibbon noted, there were more Reformed martyrs for the faith in these years than the whole Christian church produced in the amphitheaters of the ancient Empire of pagan Rome from Nero to Constantine.[48]

There is no doubt that many traditional aspects of medieval worship were rejected by the Reformed because of their associations rather than because of intrinsic faults. In Calvin's view it was right, thus, to set aside certain rites not in themselves indecorous which had become vehicles of false teaching. To cleanse the church of frightful superstitions it was necessary to remove "many ceremonies probably established of old with good reason and not notably impious of themselves."[49] But few of the extreme positions were taken by all the Reformed. Zwingli alone silenced all singing in worship, and only in Scotland were all the festivals of the church year denied. Calvin, like the ancient church, considered candles on the table unwise, but counseled the French at Wesel and Montbéliard, and the English Puritans, not to break church fellowship over them. He refused to condemn the English Prayer Book as reported to him from Frankfurt. When Hooper went to prison rather than wear vestments Calvin and Bucer sympathized with him but felt he made too much of it. Archbishop Grindal was in these things a better Calvinist. He wore popish vestments under protest to serve a greater good, but he went to prison rather than suppress the preaching of the Word. On the other hand, Calvin and other Reformers may have at times urged accommodation for practical and hopefully temporary reasons to practices they would have rejected in better times.

These liturgies must be interpreted against the background of massacre and torture, of galley slaves, kidnapped children, the wheel and gallows, the smell of burning flesh and hair. The ceremonial of their persecutors became especially distasteful to the Reformed. Those lines of robed monks chanting, the tapers, images of the Virgin, the crucifixes used to escort the martyrs to the stake, were recognized and permanently classified with devil worship. The great apostasy of the Roman Church was described in language much akin to that used in the Revelation of John in similar circumstances. The stress on human incapacity and sin and of absolute dependence on God's mercy has often seemed extreme to those of their descendants whose lines have fallen in more pleasant places. There is in these prayers no room for religious idealism or any notion that man has apart from God power either to choose or to pursue his true good. It is also true that these services seem often to argue their views; they are doctrinal and didactic. The kind of aesthetic consideration that moves most historians of liturgy did not greatly interest these churches. Their concern was for reality in worship and true obedience. We would perhaps prefer that they would gently induce a devotional mood without raising any issues that might be divisive. They preferred to know whom they trusted, and then to serve Him to the end.

V

PURITANISM AND THE ANTI-LITURGICAL MOVEMENT

LAYMEN FROM MANY REPRESENTATIVE REFORMED CHURCHES today might be somewhat disoriented by a survey of sixteenth-century Reformed liturgies. They have often been led to suppose that the characteristic worship of Reformed churches has always been "free" or "non-liturgical." Such is the pervasive influence still of an attitude that first established itself in seventeenth-century Puritanism in England and New England and Scotland. There were closely related developments in Holland, and then in Germany, Hungary, and Switzerland. The appearance and character of Reformed worship were extensively and widely changed thereby for a period of two hundred years or more, from the mid-seventeenth century to well past the middle of the nineteenth century. To this new phase we must now turn.

Puritans were not "anti-liturgical" in the sixteenth century. They were defined as a party by their attempt to continue the opposition to medieval ceremonial from earlier English Protestantism, contrary to the personal preferences of Queen Elizabeth. Images, roods, shrines, vestments, ornaments, coffin altars, gestures, the paraphernalia and gear of medieval worship, occasioned much more heat than one would have supposed they were worth. But they could be, and were in fact, used to read inacceptable theological meanings back into Prayer Book worship.

Queen Elizabeth encouraged this for political reasons, keeping alive for years the hope of a cheap conquest of Protestant England by a Catholic husband. The religious leadership of Elizabethan Anglicanism would clearly have moved in a "Puritan" direction if allowed to find its own equilibrium. In 1563 the Queen barely succeeded, with all the considerable forms of pressure at her disposal, in preventing Convocation from carrying through a series of ceremonial reforms.

The ferocious religious wars across the Channel in France and the Netherlands, and the threat of the Spanish Armada especially, increased the sensitivity to practices identified with the militant Counter-Reformation. Kneeling at Communion, the sign of the cross at Baptism, the use of the ring in marriage, seemed calculated to encourage Roman Catholic superstition. What, the Puritans demanded, were the Biblical sanctions for these practices? Anything associated with papalism was the occasion of strong emotional revulsion.

The most important single reform demanded by the Elizabethan, and indeed Jacobean, Puritans, was the preaching of the Word. Bucer and Calvin had both pressed this as a crying need back in the days of Edward, and the Puritans never gave up insisting on it. But Elizabeth was not enthusiastic about preaching. She feared and discouraged it. Four sermons a year seemed to her plenty. When the Puritans tried to develop the weekly preaching workshops, the "prophesyings," Elizabeth ordered Archbishop Grindal to suppress them. When he refused he was relieved of his functions. Hooker attempted to justify the court policy with the lame argument that the bare reading of Scripture is as effective a presentation of the Word as its preaching.

Probably the second most consistent theme of Puritan protest was the lack of discipline in the Anglican Church. The supporters of royal supremacy in the church seemed to betray a low view of the Eucharistic presence and lack of reverence for it with their "pell mell admission." There were no provisions for debarring the ignorant, irreverent, or scandalous from Communion, or for discipline generally. It was a constant theme of the Puritans as of the Reformed tradition generally to insist on the intimate relation of nurture, discipline, and worship, and Elizabethan Anglicanism was very lax in these matters.

These efforts to carry through a more consistent Reformation in England did not involve any objection to the idea of a prayer book or forms of worship as such. Many Puritans were quite content with Cranmer's work. Others who criticized the *Book of Common Prayer* simply preferred another liturgy closer to the French or Dutch Reformed type. Debates of this sort had begun among the English refugees at Frankfurt in the 1550's. There the use of spoken responses had been an issue. The repetitions of the litany and the snatches of psalm verses were disliked as artificial by those who preferred what came to be the *Book of Common Order*. Cartwright may have been the author of the "Waldegrave Liturgy" urged in Parliament in 1584 as a replacement for the *Book of Common Prayer*. This liturgy was in the Strassburg-Geneva tradition and very close to the Scottish *Book of Common Order*. A later edition was published at Middelburg in the Netherlands in 1586.[50] Both versions were disapproved by the Queen and rejected in Parliament.

But if the Elizabethan Puritans were not anti-liturgical in principle, there were a few score Separatists who were. It is in the small covenanted brotherhoods gathered by Robert Browne and Henry Barrow that we find the beginnings in England of the opposition to forms of worship as such. They play the role in England of the Anabaptists on the Continent and exhibit much the same type of worship.

The worship of the Brownists and Barrowists consisted of a congregational type of "prophesying" meeting, in which, in distinction from the usual Reformed "prophesying," there was little distinction of clergy and laity. One after another would seek to interpret and apply a given passage of Scripture. The services, often held in remote spots, might continue all day long in this fashion. Their prayers were extemporary; "one speketh and the rest doe grone, or sob, or sigh." They objected to all "stinted" (read) prayers, as muzzling the Spirit. "May such old written rotten stuff be called praier?"[51] Even the Lord's Prayer fell under this condemnation, and all sung praise, metrical or otherwise. The basic conception here was the immediate guidance of the Holy Spirit, for "if any man have not the Spirit of Christ, he is none of his. . . . Likewise the Spirit also helpeth our infirmities: for we know not what we should pray for as we ought: but the Spirit itself maketh intercession for us with groanings which cannot be uttered" (Rom. 8:9, 26). Like the Anabaptists they were extremely intolerant of the main Protestant bodies. The Brownists reprobated attendance at a *Book of Common Prayer* service as a serious sin.

A variant type of Separatist, the General or Arminian Baptists, appeared twenty years later in the reign of James I (1612). Thomas Helwys, their leader, came to believe that believers' Baptism was necessary for salvation and that the infant Baptism generally practiced by the churches left men still on the road to destruction. (Insistence on immersion did not develop until the next generation.) Adult Baptism thus generally replaced the church covenant of the Barrowists as the basis of the church. Otherwise, however, it was the same sort of gathered and disciplined congregation. The worship similarly consisted of congregational "prophesying" with free prayer. The General Baptists went a step beyond the Barrowists in using the Bible only in preparatory stages of worship, laying aside even this book then to throw themselves on the guidance of the Spirit. They were willing to permit singing by a single worshiper, but opposed congregational singing of a set form, such as the psalms. Like some Anabaptists, they apparently practiced love feasts, and footwashing, and the question of their relations with Dutch Mennonites is still debated.

Such were the congregations that first practiced "non-liturgical" worship in the English-speaking world. It is important to notice the correlation of their "free" worship with their sociological character. These are small intimate groups where everyone knows everyone else and a high level of Christian experience and knowledge is common to all. Public worship does not have here a significant evangelistic or educational role, as with a state church congregation. Here its function is rather expressive. Martin Luther had envisioned this possibility in his *German Mass*. With a congregation of "real" Christians, he said, one would have no need of elaborate liturgies, but would require only the simplest of forms. But the congregations for which he was responsible were not of this character and he found it important to provide forms of worship for them which would nurture and instruct them.

The bridge by which the non-liturgical conception of worship made its way from the sectarians into the Reformed churches was the Congregationalist Anglicans, the left wing of the Puritans. The Congregationalist tradition was born in 1618 when the first church was established in England. Under government pressure it was to develop more in Holland and New England than in England. By 1620 there were a score or so of ministers of this persuasion in Holland and several flocks. The Dutch authorities approved their request to hold their first synod there in 1621. They wished to establish a Reformed church structure with synods and classes, but with only advisory authority. The local congregation, formed with a church covenant, was conceived to hold in principle all church powers. Yet they sought to remain in communion with the Church of

England and considered the Separatists, like the General Baptists, to be schismatic. In considerable degree the Congregationalist Anglicans were simply seeking to maintain against the new centralizing state authority represented by Laud the older Elizabethan pattern of greater parish freedom in practice. John Forbes was their most aggressive leader and William Ames their chief theorist. They were high predestinarians, "Calvinist ultramontanes," supporting the positions of the Synod of Dort.

In worship the early Congregationalist Anglicans at first showed considerable variety. Many continued the practice of Elizabethan Puritans, using the Middelburg Liturgy, or an adaptation of the liturgy of their Dutch Reformed hosts. Some used the *Book of Common Prayer* and edited it. But Forbes and some other ministers used no set forms of spoken prayer, adopting in fact the Separatist conception of worship. This was to become the prevailing Congregationalist view.

Laud was not only determined to harry the Puritans out of England, but his long arm reached also to the Netherlands. Diplomatic pressure from the English government led the Dutch to require the dissolution of the Congregationalist classis there in 1635. From the Netherlands as well as from England, consequently, the Congregationalists were driven into their colonization scheme for New England. By 1630 there were few conspicuous Congregationalists left in England. In the 1640's, after the outbreak of the Civil War, several returned.

The worship of Congregationalist New England in the 1630's and 1640's is then the first firmly established practice of non-liturgical type in a Reformed church. To be sure, the New England Puritans had no scruples about congregational praise, the people's liturgy, as the General Baptists did. Even the Plymouth colony sang the metrical psalms "in course" in the Genevan manner, using Ainsworth's psalter. After the psalm, which might last as long as one half hour, Scripture was read, but not without a running commentary by the "teacher." New England would not tolerate "dumb reading." Cotton then looked for two or three "prophets" and questions. The sermon might run two or three hours, with a pause to stretch in the middle. The main prayer of thanksgiving and intercession followed the sermon in contrast to English Independency, which put the prayer *before* the sermon. One comes across such comments as that on a two-hour prayer, wishing the pastor had gone on for another hour. They stood throughout, or at least for the first hour of prayer.

The Lord's Supper was apparently celebrated monthly in New England rather than weekly as with the English Independents. All save those in full membership were to retire. The ministers and elders sat at the table, the rest remained in their pews and were served there. It was an adaptation of the à Lasco ceremonial, making it possible to serve all the congregation at once. The central Calvinist emphasis on actual communion with the risen Lord, as taught in the Westminster and Savoy Confessions, can still be read in the eighteenth-century sacramental poems of Edward Taylor, the best colonial poet.

The religious dynamic of the movement can probably be best exhibited from its preaching.[52] The great theme of Puritan preaching since the last decades of Elizabeth was personal regeneration. The Puritan preachers called for a genuine conversion of heart and life, the personal appropriation of the gospel in faith, and a life of genuine devotion amid the gross carnality of the day. Although the first two generations at least were university-trained men, they disciplined themselves deliberately to a simple, plain style, intelligible to all, avoiding the display of learning or the abstractions of philosophy. More characteristic was the psychological description of the personal drama of redemption—election, vocation, justification, sanctification, glorification. Countless journals, biographies, and autobiographies similarly illustrate this highly experiential and personalized approach to Christianity, set within an Augustinian perspective of divine initiative and grace. The practical problems of the Christian life and the disciplines of sanctification were also treated fully in sermon, catechetical sessions, and manuals of casuistry.

It was a widespread opinion among the English Puritans that a preacher should be himself a "converted" man and able to preach out of personal experience. But apparently they had not thought to make this a requirement for all lay members of the church. That was first attempted in Massachusetts Bay, where candidates must satisfy the congregation with a credible account of their personal gracious experience.[53] The Calvinist context of grace made this a different requirement from the Anabaptist or Separatist pledge of discipleship and obedience. A new "note" of the church was thus introduced in Congregationalism in New England and thence carried back to old England in the 1640's. Congregationalists, and the Calvinistic Baptists who split off from them in the 1630's, conceived the church as a fellowship of the consciously converted. And for all spoken prayer, they counted on the Holy Spirit, whom they had thus known vividly, to assist their infirmities without benefit of a book.

But while the consciousness of Christian fellowship in the gathered congregation was more intense, there was less of an awareness of the whole church of all times and places, on earth and before the throne, at worship together whenever one Christian bends his knee to God.

From another point of view, the Puritans' stress on existential immediacy affected the relation of Spirit and Word, and of the Spirit and the means of grace in general. The assumption is no longer made, as in the sixteenth century, that in the ministrations and means of the church the Spirit will normally act on the hearts of the faithful. To be sure, we should not take the extremes as characteristic, the spiritualist chaplains of Cromwell's army or the early Quakers. But the main body of Puritans still differ perceptibly from the Reformation in their tendency to dissociate in a measure God's presence from the historic ecclesiastical channels.

This new conception of Reformed worship was not widely noticed in old England until the 1640's, when the prelatical Babylon had fallen, and the Puritans had the apparent opportunity to reconstruct English Protestantism and its worship. Then the divergent tendencies and parties within Puritanism came conspicuously to view as never before.

The Directory for Worship of the Westminster Assembly[54] is the representative expression of the liturgical crosscurrents within the Puritanism of that time and must be studied from that point of view. It is also the indispensable base point from which to grasp the development of the worship of English-speaking Presbyterians, Congregationalists, and Baptists for the three centuries since that day.

The Scots Presbyterians were also influential at the Westminster Assembly, of course, and one might have supposed that they would have commended the *Book of Common Order* to its members as a model. But in fact the Scottish church had in the preceding generation developed an independent anti-liturgical tendency of its own, to parallel that of the English Puritans. Episcopacy had been superimposed on the synodical institutions of the Church of Scotland by King James, and many Scots watched jealously every attempt of the royal episcopal agents to assimilate Scottish religious practices to those of the Church of England. One now found many Scots opposed not only to the five articles forced through the General Assembly at Perth (1521) and the various liturgical drafts produced by successive commissions at royal instigation, but to set prayers as such, including their own *Book of Common*

Puritanism and the Anti-liturgical Movement   99

Order. In 1632 the Assembly felt called upon to take action against certain ministers who had dropped the "Glory be to the Father" at the end of the psalms, the affirmation of the Apostles' Creed in baptism, the ministers' private prayers at the pulpit before the service. For these innovations the Assembly threatened to depose them from the ministry. But within a decade they were to find most of the church on their side. There was thus something akin to Puritan anti-liturgical feeling in the South and West of Scotland even before the great crisis of 1637. And the attempted imposition in that year of the *Scottish Prayer Book of 1637* led to the massive revolution. The Glasgow General Assembly of 1638 defied the king and his military demonstrations, deposed his Scottish bishops, abolished episcopacy and everything now associated with it in the way of worship. The liturgical issues proper were almost entirely governed by the issue of the self-government of the church as against control by the crown through his episcopal agents. Thus the Scottish influence at the Westminster Assembly was likely to be open to some anti-liturgical suggestions. The Scots made no effort to secure the adoption of the Scottish liturgy in all three kingdoms, something which even an English Puritan like Cartwright might have wished half a century earlier.

As we turn then to the Directory for Worship, the first striking fact about the document is that it is not a liturgy or service book at all, after the fashion of Calvin, Cranmer, or Knox. As a wit has said with technical accuracy, if misleading effect, it is the only liturgy consisting of nothing but rubrics.[55] It is not a service book to be placed in the hands of all literate worshipers, but a manual for the discretionary use of ministers. And even for ministers the suggested prayers are supplied as examples only and require some verbal transpositions (readily made, to be sure) if they are to be used as set forms.

The Congregationalists and Independents had not desired any service book at all, and had no intention of using the book save by way of suggestion. Their viewpoint is clearly audible in the Preface, which, while acknowledging the need for a degree of similarity in the general heads, the sense and the scope, of public worship, and offering some help and furniture toward this end, "if need be," proceeds to warn ministers not to permit this help to encourage them to negligence in "stirring up the gifts of Christ in them." Such deep distrust of forms of prayer may also reflect fear of intolerant presbyterian authority. In any case the attitude would have astonished the Reformers of the sixteenth century.[56]

With these insistent reminders as to the freedom and responsibility of the minister, the Directory then lays out materials for a Lord's Day service in a structure recognizably of the Strassburg-Geneva pattern. But the structure could be freely reordered and other material presented, as in fact the Independents intended to do.

The Lord's Day service, it should be noted, was to be prepared and followed by the private religious exercises appropriate to the Sabbath. The Puritans generally, in contrast to the Reformers, ignored even the most basic festivals of the church calendar, but were fervent Sabbatarians, applying to the Lord's Day the Old Testament regulations for the Sabbath. Such views had not been generally held by the sixteenth-century Reformers, but spread very rapidly in England and Scotland from the turn of the century. Nicholas Bound was perhaps the single most widely influential advocate, but the general conception of the essential unity of the old and the new covenants and the encouragement of lay Bible study provided a fertile soil. The royal sponsorship of the *Book of Sports* was a calculated affront to Puritan convictions as to the manner of keeping the Lord's Day. The Westminster Confession, on the other hand, gave a classical definition of the "Christian Sabbath," and how it was to be maintained to the end of the world. Such observance was to be characteristic of the heirs of the Puritans through the eighteenth and nineteenth centuries throughout the English-speaking world. But whereas the Puritans eschewed fixed religious festivals other than the Sabbath, they frequently observed *ad hoc* fasts and thanksgivings. Their vivid sense of the immediate providential care of God was thus expressed in their reactions to disasters or blessings. Individuals set days of observance for crises in their personal lives, and congregations or whole churches observed public fasts and thanksgiving with abstinence, prayers, and psalms as appropriate. The Directory commends this practice.

For regular Sabbath worship, the Directory laid much more emphasis on the reading and exposition of Scripture than was the case with Prayer Book worship. This had been the Puritans' greatest grievance all along, as the crown consistently used the requirement of the *Book of Common Prayer* to limit or silence the pulpit. In contrast to the prayer book pericopes the Directory stipulated a full chapter from each Testament, and all Biblical books were to be worked through continuously. Thus the amount of Biblical reading suggested was about three times as extensive as in Cranmer's service. The pairing of Old Testament and New Testament was taken from the *Book of Common Order* and compares with Cranmer's Gospel and Epistle or Bucer's and Calvin's single reading.

The sermon was to be essentially expository. The Scots practiced continuous exposition, but the Independents were ready to depart more freely from the text to explore the personal drama of conversion. The Directory counseled the general Reformed practice. Preaching of the Word was viewed as "the power of God unto salvation." It presupposed "the illumination of God's Spirit, and other gifts of edification which (together with reading and studying of the Word)" a minister "ought still to seek by prayer and a humble heart." The recommended order of exposition was to proceed by the raising of the doctrinal content of the text, the adducing of "Arguments" or "Reasons," and the bringing home of the doctrine to special "use," or application to his hearers. It was this application in particular which made Puritan preaching so effective. The minister was to preach so "that his auditors may feel the word of God to be quick and powerful and a discerner of the thoughts and intents of the heart . . . that accordingly they may be quickened and excited to duty, humbled for their wants and sins, affected with their danger, and strengthened with comfort, as their condition, upon examination, shall require"; he is to choose such uses "as may most draw their souls to Christ, the fountain of light, holiness, and comfort."

The chief debate related to the use of Biblical languages and Latin in the pulpit. The Westminster Fathers assumed that a competent preacher would use them in preparation, but after debate they voted that they should not be displayed in the sermon. The preacher's task was to communicate the Word to his people, and this meant intelligibility.

There was debate as to the qualifications of preachers. The Presbyterians were uneasy about the rapid expansion of unlicensed preachers and laymen, which the Independents encouraged in congregational "prophesying." They wished also to set limits on "lecturing." "Lecturing" was a running exposition of Scripture and was especially popular through the system of Puritan "lectureships," of endowed preaching posts outside the regular benefices. The Directory permitted lecturing, but specified that if the Scripture was to be expounded, it should wait till the end of the chapter. What was merely permissive here soon became general practice. The minister added an expository "lecture" to his reading of Scripture in addition to the sermon. The Scots Assembly had to set the hour for morning worship half an hour earlier to accommodate the additional time added by the "lecturing." And the old "reader's service" disappeared altogether.

The Directory thus involved a reuniting of what had come to be the separate services of the reader and the minister. The original Reformation Lord's Day service had formed a unity, but in the last third of the sixteenth century nearly all the Reformed churches had combined the daily "reader's service" of psalms, Scripture lessons, and prayers, with the Lord's Day service of the minister, as preliminary exercises. The minister entered after the Scripture and psalms in time for the sermon, as apparently, did many of the congregation. It was probably a gain for the Lord's Day service to have one unified service led by the minister. But the loss of weekday church services was only partially compensated for by the great expansion of daily family worship characteristic of Puritanism.

The Puritan movement was associated with a sociological development of some significance, the rise of a literate middle-class laity. In contrast to the sixteenth-century situation, most members of the Puritan congregations apparently could, and did, read their own Bibles privately, along with a tremendous new devotional literature. Related to this was the transfer of daily worship from the parish church to the family. In many cases, no doubt, this transfer was affected by theological disagreements with the parish minister, but new possibilities for private nurture and worship were now at hand. The number of catechisms designed for the use of heads of families is notable. And most Puritan pastors spent considerable time in family catechizing in addition to at least one public catechization each week. Baxter expects the Christian parent to lead family prayers twice daily and to catechize on Sunday, in addition to his private prayer. That was also the expectation in colonial New England and Scotland. What proportion of heads of families did so? Half of them? A third? It is of course impossible to say, but we have many, many accounts in journals, biographies, and novels of the family worship of the Puritans and their heirs. The value of such worship in the total life of the Christian congregation is the more readily assessed today when it has almost disappeared.

To return to the Directory, and its guidelines for the spoken prayers of the minister, an opening call to worship was recommended and a prayer of adoration and confession, invoking the assistance of the Spirit, especially on the portion of Scripture to be read. Then were to follow ordinarily a chapter each from the Old Testament and the New Testament, and a psalm. The psalm might, however, be read or sung either before or after or between the lessons. The devotion to the psalter is shown by the recommendation that the psalms should also be used frequently as the basis of preaching.

In the old services of the Strassburg tradition, of course, a prayer of general confession had preceded the prayer for illumination and the Scripture. The arrangement of the prayers in the Directory is curious. It was the English Independent custom to compress nearly everything into one "long prayer" before the sermon. This is substantially the way in which the materials for prayer are set forth in the Directory. But the prayers could also be separated out and redistributed over the service. There were two pages of prayer for illumination, four pages of confession, over three pages of intercessions. These prayers could even, with slight adaptations, be used for a liturgy. They were, in fact, so printed up in liturgical form for the use of ships at sea.

The Directory did suggest that the thanksgivings be set after the sermon. The Scots also preferred the intercessions here (rather than before the sermon), as for public authorities, churches, those in distress, and special causes. To these might be added supplication for the continuance of the gospel in power, a few petitions related to the chief heads of the sermon, prayer for a preparation for "Death and

Puritanism and the Anti-liturgical Movement

Judgment and watching for the coming of our Lord Jesus Christ" and prayer for the acceptance of our worship through his intercession. The actual use of the Lord's Prayer was here commended, the Independents not pushing their opposition to it.

But the Independents did make good their opposition to the Creed, which traditionally followed this prayer. They attacked it "as an old patchery of evil stuff" and, although it was twice voted in, it was somehow lost and the Directory says nothing of it here. Rather, the service concludes with a second psalm and the blessing.

When the Lord's Supper was to be celebrated it should follow the sermon and prayer. The minister was to set forth the purpose and meaning of the Sacrament, to warn the ignorant and scandalous, to encourage the brokenhearted and scrupulous. The Assembly divines were generally agreed on the necessity of due preparation and pastoral discipline in relation to the Sacrament. In Scotland the standing practice was for a visitation of the whole congregation by the elders before Communion and the use of tokens for admission. The English Puritans similarly found one of their major grievances against Anglican practice in its lack of discipline. Apparently the Assembly's first draft on this subject was more specific, but a Parliament jealous of a new clericalism cut it back to the simple statement that "the ignorant and the scandalous are not fit to receive this sacrament," and to the minister's warning. But the Scottish Assembly specified in addition that the usual congregational examination should continue there. The Directory itself required also a preparatory service unless the Supper were to be held weekly (the apparent meaning of "frequently" here) whereby all might come better prepared to the heavenly feast.

There was no sign of sensitivity to the tense issues of the sixteenth century about the mode of the Eucharistic presence. There is even a prayer of invocation on the elements such as Cranmer had avoided in the Prayer Book of 1552 as open to misunderstanding. The Directory instructs the minister to pray God "to vouchsafe his gracious presence, and the effectual working of his Spirit in us, and so to sanctifie these Elements both of Bread and Wine, and to blesse his own Ordinance, that we may receive by faith the Body and Blood of Jesus Christ crucified for us, and so to feed upon him, that he may be one with us and we with him, that he may live in us and we in him, and to him, who hath loved us, and given himself for us."

The hottest and most extended debates at the Assembly related to its ceremonial. None approved coffin altars or the minister standing between the congregation and the table. A kneeling reception at a rail, as Laud had tried to impose it, was universally opposed. The actions at the table must be in clear view. But the Scots were deeply attached to their custom of seating the congregation at long tables in the closest imitation of the Last Supper. They also laid much weight on the custom of passing the bread and cup from hand to hand. The English, by contrast, were used to a small Communion table, from which the bread and cup were carried by the minister to the people seated in their pews or even kneeling. The English did not object to seating people at the table, but they felt it important for the Sacrament of unity that the whole congregation be served together. On the Scottish system there must be successive sittings at the table, either in the same service or on successive days. Apparently they did not consider the Huguenot procedure of coming forward and receiving standing at the table. The Directory left open both possibilities, to "sit at it, or about it," and the various groups were free to continue their several ceremonies. The Scots General Assembly added to their adoption of the Directory the proviso that Church of Scotland communicants were to receive *at* the table and to distribute the elements from one to another.[57]

Puritanism and the Anti-liturgical Movement

As with the other products of the Westminster Assembly, the Directory did not achieve the general standing originally intended for it as the standard of a uniform Reformed order in the three kingdoms of England, Scotland, and Ireland. The Scots did adopt it officially in 1645, with some further specifications. But in England, of course, it was never put into effect as the governing order of the national church. Under the relatively tolerant regime of Cromwell, congregations who desired might use it, and after the Restoration and the definitive schism of English Protestantism in 1662, the new denominations of English Presbyterians, Congregationalists, and Baptists could at least maintain this type of worship for themselves. As late as the last decade of the nineteenth century an American historian could still define the order of worship of these denominations as "essentially rigid" and recognizably related to the Directory.[58]

But in most cases the legatees of the Westminster Assembly Puritans did not care to maintain the full prescriptions of the Directory. The anti-liturgical current moved most of them still farther to the left. Perhaps the most faithful exponents of the Directory after the Restoration were the Episcopalian minority in Scotland, who were distinguished, not by the Anglican prayer book, which they did not follow, but by their use of the Lord's Prayer, the Creed, and the "Glory be to the Father" in a service modeled on the Westminster Directory. The Church of Scotland itself had by the end of the century come close to the position maintained by the Congregationalists against the Presbyterians at the Westminster Assembly. Presbyterians generally gave up the liturgical use of the Lord's Prayer, despite the recommendations of the Directory, and adopted the Congregationalist fear of the uncommented reading of Scripture. An eighteenth-century Scottish Presbyterian could get into trouble for following the instructions of the Directory as to reading Scripture and using the Lord's Prayer.[59] Even metrical psalmody suffered. The custom of "lining out," conceded by the Directory in cases "where many in the congregation cannot read," became the normal practice in Scotland and America in Presbyterian and Congregational churches.

There was a similar movement away from the Directory with regard to the Lord's Supper. The Directory had recommended "frequent" Communion. But in Scotland, particularly, where only a minority of parishes had ever been moved beyond the medieval Catholic standard of one annual Communion, even that standard seemed too high. The rigorous preparatory scrutiny by kirk sessions made the prospect formidable even when conditions were sufficiently peaceful. Glasgow saw eight Communions in the forty-five years after the Westminster Assembly.

There were some compensations, to be sure, for the rarity of celebrations. The Lord's Supper now took on the character of a regional religious festival of several days' duration for people from several parishes at once. The "Protesters" apparently developed this practice in the Cromwellian period, gathering their supporters from all congregations within traveling distance and keeping six or a dozen ministers at work preaching through the days of preparation, the actual conduct of the Sacrament on the Sunday, and the Monday of thanksgiving. These gatherings were carried on by the Covenanters in the open air and were sealed in the affections of the Scots by the martyrs associated with them in the "Killing times." They involved anywhere from one thousand to twelve thousand participants, and the actual Communion of these multitudes on the Sunday normally lasted from nine in the morning until dark. These were deeply impressive and awe-inspiring occasions in the lives of those attending. Such Communion seasons were familiar to the Presbyterians in the American colonies, and were the seedbeds of some of the great revivals. It remains true, however, that the regular worship of the church was reduced to preaching services and that little trace was left of the origin of its structure in a Mass with sermon.

Some measure of the revolution effected by the Puritan movement in Reformed worship can be seen in the contrast with the French experience. When the storm troopers of the Counter-Reformation drove the Huguenots by the thousands into exile abroad in the 1680's, many were brought into contact with the churches of England and her American colonies. Although they were scarcely prepared to accept the Arminianism introduced by the court into Anglicanism in the 1620's and virtually official since the Restoration, they found the worship of the English Presbyterians and Congregationalists equally alien. In worship, the *Book of Common Prayer* seemed closer to the Calvinist heritage than did anti-liturgical Puritanism.

And what happened to the Puritan style of worship when the Spirit no longer made himself powerfully felt? Intense and powerful as it doubtless was in the first half of the seventeenth century, "non-liturgical" worship itself became a form, a tradition, by the end of the century. As such it could then become as mechanical, formal, and tedious as could the use of the *Book of Common Prayer*. Not that it always did. We should probably take Isaac Watts's *Guide to Prayer* as a model of the best practice of non-liturgical worship in the Presbyterian, Congregationalist, and Baptist churches of the eighteenth and nineteenth centuries. But here we have the picture of an intelligent and devout discipline for the leader of public worship rather than the original abandonment to the inbreaking Spirit. And the demands made on the gifts and training of such a minister were such as to qualify him for a denominational liturgical commission. There were such men, but the mine-run were not so well equipped for their ministry.

For two centuries or more the arguments were rehearsed

for and against set forms, with little novelty. The rival patterns had each its superior utility for certain types of situations and congregations and neither had universal superiority. And as for authenticity of worship, this is not secured either by forms or by their rejection, but in either case is the gift of God.

VI

PIETISM AND EVANGELICALISM: THE EXPERIENCE OF CONVERSION

PIETISM AND EVANGELICALISM, LIKE PURITANISM BEFORE them, were attempts at religious renewal within Protestantism. The Reformation seemed to have been only partially successful, a necessary reform of church institutions, doctrines, practices, but which had not yet borne fruit adequately in Christian life. The various Pietist movements, like Puritanism, were originally oriented polemically against the formal orthodoxy and institutionalism of the established Protestant churches, not on theological or ecclesiastical grounds but in the name of deeper devotion and a more dedicated life. Such renewal was desperately needed. The wars of the seventeenth century, especially the Dutch War for Independence, the Thirty Years' War in the Germanies, and the Civil War in England, had left their usual legacy of spiritual and moral exhaustion and the brutalization of life. Religion in many quarters survived only as a matter of doctrinal orthodoxy and external observance, maintained by partisan and unedifying preaching. The morals of clergy as well as laity were often deplorable. There may be some lack of balance, e.g., in the "black legend" found in some Wesleyan literature about Anglican conditions in the first third of the eighteenth century, but there was only too much basis for it in fact. Conditions were probably worse in some parts of the Continent. A new emphasis on personal appropriation of religion and serious religious practice was the essential concern of all the movements we have to describe.

Perhaps the most characteristic trait of all these movements, and one they shared with Puritanism, was the normative place in the Christian life which they assigned to a felt conversion experience with its sense of assurance of salvation. The emphasis on a subjective emotional experience necessarily affected the classical Reformation focus on Word and Sacraments in the historic church as the loci and media of salvation. Many of the early Pietists and Puritans were strong churchmen (the radical Separatists were always in a minority), but the new subjective and individualist orientation made even the conservative Pietist or Evangelical sit somewhat freer to the institutional church and her means of grace than had the classical Protestant.

Conversion experience understood as normative for the Christian has often been defined as a characteristic trait of Puritanism in old and New England. But whereas the Puritan hoped to shape a holy commonwealth and culture around this conception of the Christian life, the Pietist accepted a more modest hope. Or, rather, he generally postponed to the day of the Lord's Return (which for him was often a vivid expectation) the fulfillment of the reign of the saints, while leading a somewhat introverted life, largely withdrawn from politics and many worldly interests. His aggressiveness for the Kingdom was often channeled into an ardent evangelism of individuals, at home and abroad, for his type of conversion experience. So defined, Pietism or Evangelicalism might be conceived as a Puritanism individualized and no longer ambitious of political and cultural dominance. Classical Puritanism, we might say, effectively ended with the Restoration of the Stuarts and Laudian episcopacy in England, and what endured of the central thrust after a generation or two of adjustment, was Evangelicalism and Pietism. On the

Pietism and Evangelicalism   113

Continent, meanwhile, the comparable movements were never in sight of power in any such way as were the English Puritans in the mid-seventeenth century, and the program in the Netherlands, Germany, Switzerland, Hungary was always Pietist rather than Puritan. In this chapter the weight will lie on the first century or two of the Pietist and Evangelical movements, but the tradition is still a living force in the mid-twentieth century. In the nature of the case we will describe, not the reconstruction of basic institutions, but efforts of representative individuals and groups to reanimate or supplement inherited patterns.

The influence of English Puritanism was conspicuous across the North Sea in the growth of what was to become known as Pietism or Precisianism in the Dutch Reformed Church. The two most conspicuous exponents at the time of the Synod of Dort (1618–1619) were Willem Teelinck and William Ames, the latter a native Englishman. Teelinck, a lawyer, was converted while visiting in England, where he lived some time with devout Puritans of the school of Arthur Hildersam and John Dod. He came back to the Netherlands, in the first years of James's reign, bringing strict Sabbatarianism, devout household prayers three times a day, weekly catechizing, the practice of frequent private fasts. He became a pastor, and in his service at Middelburg from 1613 to 1629 changed the religious practice of that city.

Teelinck was loyal to the confessions and opposed to the Remonstrants. But he contended that formal orthodoxy was not enough, that a reformation of life must follow the sixteenth-century reformation of doctrine. He found himself compelled to debate even with the high predestinarians on these grounds. In Middelburg he preached to crowded assemblies, and used his weekly catechetical sessions in such fashion that many adults attended with the children. He catechized also in homes through the week. Other regular religious meetings for men and for women were established. For the use of such informal and domestic worship he composed and published catechetical materials, books of prayers, his own religious journal. Only the truly reborn, he argued, should be admitted to the pastoral office. And his whole energy was selflessly devoted to preaching and teaching genuine repentance and conversion to all whom he could reach.

There was a strong ascetic note in Teelinck. He practiced private fasts frequently. He preached and wrote against display and luxury in the dress of Christians. Joined with this was a new charitable and evangelistic zeal. He furthered various charitable enterprises and in his *Ecce Homo* of 1622 raised the first notable call to foreign missions in the Reformed Church.

William Ames, meanwhile, found his chief center of influence at Franeker, where he taught theology from 1622 to his death in 1633. He conceived of theology, like his Cambridge teacher Perkins, as a practical discipline, as living to God, the pursuit of devotion. There was no doubt of his formal orthodoxy; he served as a special aide to Bogerman, the president of the Synod of Dort. But Scholasticism was to serve the inner life of religion. He formulated the classical Congregationalist view of the church as a covenanted company of the converted. His death prevented his migration to Massachusetts Bay, where, it has been maintained, he would have been acknowledged as pope.[60] These ideas were to be most freely actualized in New England, but they were to be felt in many Continental Reformed churches as well.

Gisbert Voet was the most conspicuous Dutch representative of this union of Scholastic orthodoxy and personal devotion for the middle generation of the century. He was deeply influenced by Teelinck, and likewise experienced the personal and family piety of English Puritanism at first hand. He sponsored a Dutch translation of Bayly's *Practice of Piety* and several volumes of devotional and ascetic

Pietism and Evangelicalism 115

writings, including many Roman Catholic authors. As professor of theology at Utrecht for some forty years he exercised a widespread influence on the Dutch church.

By the middle of the century the Pietist current was already strong in the Netherlands. The country was flooded with devotional and ascetic literature, including translations of many English Puritans. Family worship was universally insisted on as the key to the reformation of Christian life in the church and increasingly replaced the Reformation weekday services in the church building. Strict Sabbatarianism was characteristic. Domestic catechizing meetings were well established. Asceticism in amusements, abstention from cards, dancing, fairs, was widely observed, as well as private fasting. One found even occasional celibates. Stricter church discipline was demanded, at times running to extremes, as when Lodensteyn vowed not to celebrate the Lord's Supper again, so distressed was he by its profanation.

An epoch in the development of this Continental Puritanism or Pietism was signalized by the startling career of the former Jesuit, Jean de Labadie. The Pietists of Middelburg called him from Geneva in 1666. In Geneva he had had great success with informal worship conducted in homes and he began this practice at once on a daily schedule in Middelburg. It was a form of congregational "prophecy," based on a free exposition and application of Scripture, for laity as well as the clergy. Labadie had marked gifts for free prayer, which he always used, and was able to carry congregations with him to the heavenly presence. Thus the conventicle style of worship, already widespread in the Netherlands, was transferred over to regular Lord's Day worship. This tendency was already apparent at Middelburg before Labadie's arrival. The weekday services had already eliminated all set prayers except the opening "Our help is in the name of the Lord," and the Lord's Prayer. But Labadie made this general and systematic. Only free prayer was worthy of a genuinely Christian congregation and a truly converted pastor.

Labadie's efforts at constituting a congregation solely of converted Christians quickly ran into difficulties. After only four years in Middelburg he was deposed from his ministry and forced to change his ecclesiastical strategy. He decided that the reform he sought could not be effected in any territorial church, but must rather grow out of voluntary association. The later adventures of the Labadist communities in Holland, North America, and North Germany need not concern us. But their indirect influence on Dutch and German Pietists was important for the rest of the century. They worked in a separatist direction. The conventicles of the regenerate were frequently highly critical of the parish congregations and their pastors. Hundreds and thousands of Pietists refused any longer to attend Communion in the parish churches with those of less intense piety. Some refused to pray the Lord's Prayer with the unconverted, since God is truly "Father" only of the converted. Some Pietist pastors would not permit the use of the Lord's Prayer when (unconverted) children were present. It was assumed by the followers of Labadie that the regenerate had the gift of testing the religious quality and experience of others. Not all the Pietists were so confident of this. But Pietists generally were persuaded that set prayers were appropriate only to unconverted nominal Christians. By the first generation of the eighteenth century such pietism was strong if not dominant in all provinces and classes, if not all congregations, of the Dutch Reformed Church.

Pietism appeared in the German Reformed Church chiefly through Dutch, and indirectly, English Puritan influences. The chief Reformed area, the Palatinate, had been devastated by the Thirty Years' War and then later in the century by the Mongolian ferocity of Louis XIV. The most important remaining Reformed centers were on

Pietism and Evangelicalism

the lower Rhine and in scattered communities like Bremen. Here were felt the influence of Voet, Lodensteyn, Labadie from about 1670.

Even before that time Untereyck was utilizing conventicles on the Dutch model at Mülheim. He had studied with Voet at Utrecht and had visited English Puritans on the eve of the Restoration there. His long pastorate was to be in the seaport of Bremen from 1670. He was very successful in the use of informal gatherings for Bible study in his home after service and during the week. Frau Untereyck had similar meetings for women and for children. She introduced regular weekly catechizing of children in Bremen and eventually, a regular procedure of confirmation as its consummation. Untereyck used free prayer rather than the Palatinate order and declined to follow the lectionary pericopes as, under Lutheran influence, was the Bremen custom. He wished to strengthen discipline and especially to fence the Lord's Supper, but was not so arbitrary as Nethenus and Copper in Meurs, who were both deposed because of their refusal to administer the Sacrament in the absence of communicants worthy in the pastor's estimation.

Joachim Neander, the pioneer of Reformed hymnody, was converted by Untereyck in 1670. He taught in a Latin school at Düsseldorf and conducted conventicles there like those of Untereyck. In the meantime he was writing his *Hymns of the Covenant,* which were first published in 1679. His hymns were not intended for church worship but for prayer meetings and home worship, and for some years their use was confined to such informal occasions. They did enrich and strengthen the worship of the German Pietists, Lutheran as well as Reformed. "Praise ye the Lord, the Almighty, the King of Creation!" "O Thou True God Alone," and "All My Hope Is Fix'd and Grounded" are of the few known in translation in the English-speaking world. Neander himself died at thirty before he became famous, only a year after he was called, in 1679, to join Untereyck in Bremen.

F. A. Lampe was also to be associated with Bremen. He was converted at Franeker and drawn within the influence of Lodensteyn and Untereyck. After pastorates at Duisburg and Bremen he became professor of theology at Utrecht in 1720. He put even more emphasis on his catechetical work, his prayer meetings, and his house-to-house visitation than on his preaching. He developed from the notion of "testing the spirits" a rather elaborate classification of spiritual conditions. These were practically important; when he addressed himself specifically to the converted in his sermons, they would rise in their seats. Like many of the Pietists, he preached the imminent Second Coming. His massive series on the *Mystery of the Covenant of Grace* (1712–1721, in six volumes) qualified him as the leading theologian of his church. He also composed a number of hymns.

The penetration of Pietist worship practices into the German Reformed churches can be measured by synodical legislation.[61] Prayer meetings and conventicles were generally accepted within the framework of parish life, but numerous regulations were laid down. Additions to, or variants of, the prayers of the Palatinate order were first permitted by the General Synod of 1677. The Synod of Berg in 1728 forbade any further modifications by preachers or by particular synods. The old formularies were printed as late as 1770, but local practice was by that time very variable, with free prayer dominant. The first version of the psalter to include hymns was that of 1736. The Prussian king pushed the book in his territories. But the preference for psalms was tenacious and the new book was not universally accepted even in 1773, when a new translation of the psalter with a hymn supplement was commended by the General Synod. Organs made their way back into the churches in the course of the eighteenth

Pietism and Evangelicalism

century. The synods repeatedly and vainly attempted to discourage the practice of private Baptism and similarly complained of the growing neglect of Communion. Both Sacraments suffered from the influence of Pietism, although the early Pietists had held them in great respect. Confirmation, conceived as personal acceptance of the baptismal covenant, came to be stressed more than the act of Baptism itself. And the rigorous qualifications insisted upon for Communion, as with the Roman Catholic Jansenists, made for an infrequent celebration.

English and Dutch "Puritan" influences were also significant in mid-seventeenth-century Reformed Hungary. They were felt in a dual protest against episcopacy and against the liturgical tradition of sung Mass. The most conspicuous leader, János Tolnai Dali, came under the influence of the father of Congregationalism, William Ames, at the Dutch university of Franeker in the 1630's. He and ten others went from the Netherlands to London. In 1638 they founded a society there to presbyterianize the Reformed Church of Hungary. When Tolnai returned to Hungary he became dean and professor and won a considerable following.

In the event the Hungarian Puritans lost their struggle against episcopacy. Tolnai and eight other ministers were deposed in 1646 at a National Council at Szatmárnémeti.[62] Others continued the struggle for a time but unsuccessfully. But Tolnai's party largely won the battle against ritual and form in worship, despite the support given by George Rákóczy I, a Calvinist, to the fuller forms. Two Reformed bishops, János Keserü Dajka and István Geleji Katona, had just published in 1636 the "Big Graduale," a collection of liturgical materials of the sung Mass type. But the Reformers expunged the responses and antiphons and refused to be bound by the pericopes of the church calendar. Even the Lord's Prayer became rare as a congregational act. One characteristic ceremonial remained, the congregation rose for the Scripture, and sometimes for the invocation and opening hymn, and the benediction. The substance of Hungarian worship came to be the Word preached and spoken prayers by the minister, with congregational praise from Molnár's beautiful Hungarian metrical psalms.

Pietism in Switzerland was relatively late, and more influenced at first by German Lutheranism than by the Reformed movements of Great Britain or the Netherlands. There were prayer meetings in the 1690's in Berne in which the authorities were irritated by the criticism of unconverted ministers and undisciplined congregations, as well as by the use of Swiss German in sermons and the disregard of social distinctions in the meetings. These were suppressed, but not before the conversion of Samuel Lutz, who was to continue evangelistic prayer meetings and catechization in the Bernese Oberland for most of the first half of the eighteenth century.

In the early eighteenth century the Swiss Pietist movements seemed to tend toward separatist or radical extremes. Perhaps it was the influence of foreign separatists, Quakers, Philadelphians, the Camisard "Inspired," or various German radicals. Perhaps it was the relative hostility of the church leaders. Not until the second half of the century did Swiss Pietism find itself a constructive role generally within the churches. It was in part the Moravian fellowship that provided a new institutional base. D'Annoni of Basel was one of those influenced by the Moravians. He encouraged home prayer meetings, the use of Swiss German in worship, and a hymnal to be used with Lobwasser's psalter. Toward the end of the eighteenth century the "Christianity Society," centered in Basel, displayed the same denominational indifference seen among the English Evangelicals. In this case, of course, it meant fellowship between Lutherans and Reformed. The large-scale development of Swiss Pietism, however, waited for the Awakening after the French Revolution.

Pietism and Evangelicalism

The "renewed" Church of the Moravians, or Unity of Brethren, was a unique religious order which made itself widely felt in mid-eighteenth-century Protestantism. We have seen how the heirs of the Hussites, the Bohemian Brethren, had allied themselves with both Lutheran and Reformed groups in the Consensus of Sendomir. After their rebirth from apparent annihilation in the Thirty Years' War they were to play a similar ecumenical role.

A few refugees from the terrorism of the Hapsburg Counter-Reformation were the seedbed for a renewal in which even their episcopal succession was maintained. Having fled over the mountains from Bohemia, they were permitted to settle on undeveloped land in Saxony on the estate of Count von Zinzendorf, a devout Lutheran Pietist. There at Herrnhut the Moravian congregation was allowed to shape its own traditional church life within the context of the Lutheran state church parish. The count, who desired to be a patron of such Pietist missionary and philanthropic institutions as those at Halle, found it necessary to make concessions to the institutions of the Brethren in order to persuade them to stay. Increasingly impressed with their traditions, he fused his Lutheran Pietism with their evangelical zeal and became their religious leader as well as protector.

The peculiar monastic institutions of the Moravian settlements, first at Herrnhut and later at other centers, developed in considerable measure out of their practical exigencies as refugees. Housing and employment were organized on a communal basis, with family life subordinated. There were dormitories for single men, single women, and married couples. Each came to have its own religious as well as economic and educational life, so that the whole community was organized into "choirs" based on age, sex, and marital status. Each choir, in turn, was subdivided into cells, or *Bänden,* of from three to six members, who maintained by daily mutual sharing an intimate religious fellowship. Choirs and bands had regular religious exercises, with "love feasts" and litanies. The whole community met daily three times for worship and Sunday was wholly devoted to that purpose.

The devotional orientation of these various worshiping groups was directed to continuous personal fellowship with the personal Savior, each choir focusing on the appropriate stage or relation in Jesus' life. The mode was emotional, imaginative, sensuous, with a minimum of intellectual structure. Zinzendorf differed from the Halle type of Pietism, as represented by Francke or, in America, by Muhlenberg, and from the comparable Reformed Pietism of Whitefield and Tennent, in his disregard of the crisis of condemnation and repentance. He had never had such a datable conversion himself and maintained the sense of assurance through intense preoccupation with the blood and wounds of Jesus.

In this, Moravianism marked a shift in the polemic orientation of Pietism. Earlier Puritanism and Pietism was a movement for more thoroughgoing reform, especially in personal devotion and discipline, as against a Protestantism tending to dead orthodoxy. But in the eighteenth century the situation changed. The danger was now less that from formalism and mere orthodoxy than from mere moralism. The blood and wounds of Moravianism emphasized just those aspects of the faith disliked by the rationalists, the sacrificial atonement of Jesus Christ, the Son of God. Similarly, John Wesley was to stress grace and forgiveness in an Anglican church which had lapsed to preaching mere ethics.

The language of the Moravian hymns and litanies, especially in the "sifting time" of the 1740's, mingled erotic symbolism and devotion to blood in a fashion offensive to many ears, at times running to barely coherent religious baby talk. The Lord's Supper was described as the embrace of the Husband, and the congregation dwelt in pious fantasy

Pietism and Evangelicalism

> Within our Husband's pierced side
> Where all his little hearts abide.[63]

The extremes of devotion to the bloody sweat, the nail prints, the side's cleft opened wide for the faithful, were edited out in time and the central thrust of Moravian piety is well represented by Toplady's hymn:

> Rock of Ages, cleft for me,
> Let me hide myself in Thee;
> Let the water and the blood,
> From Thy riven side which flowed,
> Be of sin the double cure,
> Cleanse me from its guilt and power.

The worship of the Moravian community was sustained by almost continuous music. Preaching was little emphasized, or even Bible-reading. The famous daily devotional texts, the *Losungen,* which bound together their adherents around the world, were themes for the daily singing meetings. These services were dominated by the "hymn sermons," in which, after the fashion of a "picked" psalm in Puritanism, the minister would lead off in one stanza after another from different hymns in endless combinations, the organist and congregation joining in after the first phrase or two. The communities knew hundreds of hymns by heart and sang without books. Hymns were composed by the tens of thousands, but no hymnbook can convey the actual practice. Their trombone choirs were also characteristic, as when sounding solemnly from the belfry the hymns that marked the death of a member, or in ringing out the Easter faith in the litany at dawn in the cemetery. Men walked to and from work in the fields to trumpets, and even the night watchmen marked the hours, not with "All's well" but with hymn verses. The musical culture of the Moravian settlements in the American colonies was a world above that of all the surrounding churches of English background.

In this close-knit and all-absorbing community life there was a great variety of special services, love feasts, footwashings, vigils, as at New Year's Eve, and elaborate litanies, such as the Easter Litany, the Communion Litany, the Great Church Litany. An hourly intercession was maintained around the clock, for over a century, and special conference meetings, both oriented particularly to the missionaries in the West Indies, Greenland, Pennsylvania, and elsewhere. Part of the congregation was constituted of men ready at any time to undertake assignment overseas. At the indication of the lot they would respond in the spirit of the hymn of the original refugees,

> Blessed be the day when I must roam
> Far from my country, friends and home,
> An exile, poor and mean.[64]

For decades the Moravians carried the lion's share of Protestant missions.

The Moravian fellowship had two social forms. There were the monastic settlements, like Herrnhut, Marienborn, Herrnhaag, Fulneck, Fairfield, Gracehill, Bethlehem, Nazareth, Lititz, Salem. Related to these was a "diaspora" of awakened souls in the surrounding established churches, who drew religious sustenance from Moravian piety but functioned within their own religious institutions. In this fashion members of Reformed churches in Switzerland, France, Germany, and elsewhere were at the same time members of the "invisible" Church of Jesus in the Moravian conception. In the English-speaking world with its liberty for religious association, Zinzendorf noted, there was less occasion for this peculiar pattern. There the Methodist movement was to develop new institutional patterns for disseminating many Moravian views and practices.

As we turn to the Evangelicalism of the English-speaking world, the most conspicuous manifestation in worship is the introduction of hymns. The greatest single individual factor, to be sure, was Isaac Watts, who was not an Evangelical, and who even developed Arian leanings later in life. But Watts stabilized the character of the English hymn and effectively argued the case for its liturgical use.

Most early English hymn writers of the seventeenth and eighteenth centuries intended hymns for informal use outside the regular services of the church. So it was with the Wesleys and the authors of the Olney hymns. But Watts challenged the whole system of metrical psalmody head on in the preface to his *Hymns and Spiritual Songs* (1707). The church needed vehicles of her specifically Christian faith which the Old Testament did not provide. And the church should voice her own praise to God, rather than using the language of God's revelation to man. To illustrate his case Watts supplied some 210 hymns in the first edition. They were not generally "pietistic" in the nineteenth-century sense, but rather corporate, historical, cosmic in scope, like the liturgical psalms. The language and imagery was Scriptural, but adapted to the mind of the living church. In fact they were not very different from the *Psalms of David Imitated in the Language of the New Testament,* the sequel Watts supplied a dozen years later. For Watts reworked the sentiments of the psalms for the eighteenth-century church, achieving, by his cultural translation, much the end result to which the sixteenth century came by its more flexible exegesis. Not all the psalms, he felt, could be made suitable, so he retained but 138 of the 150.

A score or more of Watts's Christian psalms are still part of the living liturgy and a sampling will be recalled at once.

> From all that dwell below the skies
> Let the Creator's praise arise ...

> Our God, our Help in ages past,
> Our Hope for years to come ...

> Before Jehovah's awful throne,
> Ye nations, bow with sacred joy . . .
>
> Begin, my tongue, some heavenly theme,
> And speak some boundless thing . . .
>
> Jesus shall reign where'er the sun
> Does his successive journeys run . . .
>
> Joy to the world! the Lord is come:
> Let earth receive her King . . .
>
> When I survey the wondrous cross
> On which the Prince of Glory died . . .
>
> Alas! and did my Saviour bleed,
> And did my Sovereign die! . . .
>
> Come, Holy Spirit, heavenly Dove,
> With all Thy quickening powers . . .
>
> There is a land of pure delight
> Where saints immortal reign . . .

To these should be added two or three from Doddridge, Watts's friend and protégé:

> O God of Bethel, by whose hand
> Thy people still are fed . . .
>
> My God, and is Thy table spread
> And does Thy cup with love o'erflow? . . .
>
> Awake, my soul, stretch every nerve,
> And press with vigor on . . .

The use of Watts's hymns was a theme of controversy for over a century, and there were secessions in more than one Reformed country as late as the nineteenth century on the issue of hymnody vs. psalmody. But the "three old denominations" whose representative ministers bore Watts's body to the grave were all in time won over and a third of Wesley's first hymnal came from Watts.

Pietism and Evangelicalism

John Wesley is perhaps the most famous representative of eighteenth-century English Evangelicalism. Wesley's momentous meeting with the Moravian emigrants to the colonies in 1736 is a much-told story which explains his passage from an overscrupulous "Catholic" piety to Pietist conversionism and the experience of assurance. On his return to England he visited the Moravian settlements in Germany, as his *Journal* records, and he took his own new start in England in 1738 in a Moravian society in London. His "societies," "classes," "bands" were designed on the Moravian model to facilitate close and constant mutual supervision of all members and to provide a sphere of lay ministry. Here were to be used the quarterly love feasts, and watch nights, the latter at first monthly, and then, as with the Moravians, on New Year's Eve, along with the covenant service adapted from Puritan antecedents.

In the Band and Society meetings, again, were developed the most characteristic aspects of Methodist worship, the tradition of free prayer and the use of the Methodist hymns. Neither was conceived as appropriate for formal Anglican parish worship, constituted by prayer book liturgy and metrical psalms. The dozens of booklets of hymns published by the Wesleys were taught in the Society meetings, lined out two lines at a time. Anthems were not permitted and instruments were rarely used. John Wesley had been much affected by Moravian congregational hymn-singing and hoped to emulate it. The hymns of Charles Wesley in fact became the greatest literary achievement of the Evangelical movement, ranked by some critics with the *Book of Common Prayer* and the psalms themselves.[65] A handful of opening lines must suffice to recall their riches:

> O for a thousand tongues to sing
>   My great Redeemer's praise ...
> Ye servants of God, your Master proclaim,
>   And publish abroad His wonderful Name ...

Come, Thou long-expected Jesus,
    Born to set Thy people free . . .

Rejoice, the Lord is King:
    Your Lord and King adore! . . .

Love divine, all loves excelling,
    Joy of heaven, to earth come down . . .

Jesus, Lover of my soul,
    Let me to Thy bosom fly . . .

Christ, whose glory fills the skies,
    Christ the true, the only Light . . .

Hark! the herald angels sing,
    "Glory to the new-born King" . . .

Jesus Christ is risen today, Alleluia!
    Our triumphant holy day, Alleluia! . . .

"Christ the Lord is risen today," Alleluia!
    Sons of men and angels say; Alleluia! . . .

Soldiers of Christ, arise,
    And put your armor on . . .

Victim Divine, Thy grace we claim
    While thus Thy precious Death we show . . .

Methodist worship is a particularly clear case of a process repeated again and again in the history of Christian worship, from New Testament times. Practices originating as informal supplements to the traditional worship often came in time to have greater meaning in fact and then influenced or even replaced the established forms. Thus Wesley presupposed regular Anglican parish worship and instructed his Society members to attend there. Methodists in Wesley's lifetime far exceeded the conventional Anglican practice of three or four annual Communions, and Wesley himself communicated three or four times a week. But few of the new members gathered in had his personal sense of indebtedness to the Church of England, and Anglican clergy put great difficulties in the way of Methodist communicants. Nineteenth-century Methodism exhibited little of Wesley's Eucharistic piety and quite substituted conversionism for his own somewhat ambiguous views on baptismal regeneration. Wesley's abridged *Sunday Service of the Methodists in North America* (1784),[66] conforming as it did to many of the Puritan requisites of 1661, was still too formal for his followers, and like the Westminster Directory, was far overpassed in the direction of free discretion for the individual minister. In English city churches, especially in London, the *Book of Common Prayer*, or Wesley's abridgment, retained some hold. But the general tendency in the nineteenth century in England, and even more in America, was against both formal orders, which to most Methodists seemed artificial and unreal in comparison with the services they had learned to live from spiritually in their societies. Apart from the Sacraments and special offices Methodist worship in the nineteenth century was distinguishable from the "non-liturgical" services of the Presbyterians, Congregationalists, and Baptists only by its greater informality.

Methodism was only one distinctive nuance in the great "awakenings" of the middle generation of the eighteenth century in England, Wales, and the American colonies. Whitefield was more typical and might be taken as the representative figure for the English-speaking world. He was, of course, an Anglican, but there were powerful currents of the same sort within the three old denominations of English Nonconformity—the Presbyterians, Congregationalists, and Baptists—as well as in the churches of Wales and Scotland. In the colonies Congregationalists and Presbyterians, the two strongest churches, were both split by the Awakening, into "Old Lights" and "New," or "Old Side" and "New." The American Baptists as a denomination were virtually created in and by the Awakening. The English Independents, similarly, experienced a second spring in the late eighteenth century. In all these forms the experience of evangelical conversion was made the norm and fulcrum of the Christian life, with its consequences for worship.

Converted laymen were capable of a fluency and freedom in prayer unusual elsewhere. The private prayer and the family prayers of Evangelicals were the characteristic expression of this form of religion. It was well said that Evangelicalism is the religion of the home. Thornton's *Family Prayers* ran through thirty editions in two years. Wilberforce prayed daily for three hours, at each of 5:00 A.M., 12:00 noon, and 5:00 P.M. The effective practice of free prayer in public presupposes such habits on the part of minister and layman alike.

What was most novel in this English-speaking awakening was field preaching, the basis of what came to be called the "revival meeting." Apparently Howel Harris began it in Wales, but Whitefield and Wesley carried it everywhere. It cost Wesley a wrench, as a University fellow, accustomed to think it almost a sin to save a man outside a church building. Zinzendorf never did conquer his distaste for revival "mobs." But once Wesley began, he never faltered in a lifelong campaign of preaching conversion to those beyond the reach of the established church. It was noticed that itinerant preachers had limited success in settled communities which were adequately churched. But in the early days of industrialization in England, and on the American frontier, there were large numbers of uprooted people with long-forgotten memories of religious nurture from childhood. To reach them was not evangelism in the strict sense, but literally a "revival," a recovering of those once touched by Christianity but then unchurched in the great social movements of the time.

The revival thus became a new type of special or occasional service, often drawing on a considerable geographical area and sometimes reaching the members of several congregations. In considerable degree it was assimilated into the program of churches also. The goal of the oratory and the singing was to bring individuals to a personal decision. Various devices were developed in the nineteenth century, of preaching at or praying for individuals by name, or inviting those under conviction of guilt to "come forward" and sit on an anxious bench or a mourners' bench. In the hands of a series of revivalists, the institution became highly formalized, even "liturgical," with ritual intonations and phrases, and congregational responses. There was a wide range in cultural level, of course, from solemn churchly revivals in Anglican or Congregational parishes to the wilder frontier "camp meetings" or those of the Primitive Methodists in England, with barks, jerks, and other hysterical expressions.

From the viewpoint of the participant, "conversion" was often dramatized in a personal decision, commitment, or pledge. The form varied, but in one way or another, an individual took a definite step before witnesses in his religious and moral life. Sometimes a specific vow, as of abstinence from alcohol, would symbolize his total commitment, as a monk might undertake celibacy. Or it might be the readiness to become a foreign missionary, or to free his slaves.

Revival preachers were known by their various styles. Some were primarily sons of thunder, preachers of judgment, and the terrors of the law. Others laid more weight on forgiveness and divine mercy. Whitefield and most Anglican Evangelicals were predestinarian; Wesley was not. The relations to the established local congregations also varied. Sometimes, where there was revivalist preaching against the dangers of an unconverted ministry, relations would be strained. Some revivalists were scrupulous to work with the local ministers, to use their support in the revival and to attempt to strengthen their congregations. Many communities on the American frontier really date the substantial origins of congregational life from such revivals.

The enduring effect of the revival was usually largely governed by the degree to which its excitement was canalized in the familiar group life of Pietism, the "house meetings," the meetings for women, for children, catechizing, and, in the nineteenth century, the great proliferation of Bible societies, missionary societies, Sabbath schools, and the like.

Revivalism, presupposing a largely unconverted audience, developed a different style of praying and preaching from those appropriate to a congregation assumed to be Christian. George Whitefield probably did more than anyone else to change the style of the English and American pulpit in this way. One recalls the effect on Jonathan Edwards, who had previously delivered his carefully reasoned doctrinal sermons while staring at the bell rope. Lay exhorters sometimes got quite out of hand. Something similar happened to the prayers and the hymns. Whitefield's prayers were frankly hortatory. Neander was converted by such a prayer. And in sung praise it was apparently chiefly the Great Awakening that carried Watts to triumph in the American Congregational and Presbyterian churches. The story is told of how Jonathan Edwards returned to Northampton in the Awakening to find everyone singing Watts. After some discussion he agreed to the use of one hymn each Sabbath. At the turn of the century the Presbyterians joined the Congregationalists in sponsoring "Dwight's Watts." On a more popular level, of course, came the camp-meeting hymn and then, late in the nineteenth century, the gospel hymn as a kind of religious folk song.

The eighteenth-century Awakening was largely a phenomenon of Great Britain and her colonies. After the

Napoleonic Wars, however, similar social conditions developed on the Continent, and there, too, were experienced a series of *Erweckungen* and *réveils*. Often the nuclei were cells of the Moravian diaspora, but the attempt at a wider outreach was new.

The Anglo-American Evangelicalism, in particular, was the backbone of nineteenth-century Protestant foreign missions. When such missionaries confronted peoples of alien culture some of the limitations of "non-liturgical" worship became apparent. On the mission field one could no longer assume a heritage of generations steeped in the psalter and hymnals, in the Bible and the great themes and forms of Christian prayer. Here there was no half-forgotten Christian faith to be kindled by an ardent "revivalist." Free worship in such circumstances proved singularly inadequate for education and nurture, and often produced irreverence and crudity. The problem became more general in the twentieth century, as the erosion of Christian influence made most formerly "Christian countries" increasingly into mission fields themselves.

VII

MORALISM, RATIONALIST OR SENTIMENTAL

THE DRAMATIC CHANGES IN COSMOLOGY AND THE VIEW of man that occurred in the seventeenth century could not but affect Christian worship along with theology. The mathematical-mechanical world view of Descartes and Newton was to replace almost completely the old panpsychic cosmic hierarchy of the ancient and medieval mind. The striking practical and technological uses of the new outlook ensured its continued predominance over the imagination of the modern West.

What would this mean for the language of Christian worship, where the stage setting, at least, of the Christian story had been shaped by the obsolete cosmology? What room was there in Pascal's universe for the celestial hierarchy,

> Ye watchers and ye holy ones,
> Bright seraphs, cherubim, and thrones, ...
> ... dominions, princedoms, powers,
> Virtues, archangels, angels' choirs ... ?

What was conveyed to minds shaped by modern theories of matter and energy by transubstantiation or consubstantiation? or the root metaphors of "begotten, not made" or "Light of Light"? The language of worship, to be sure, is affirmative and evocative rather than analytical or critical. Changes there come less by way of explicit rejection than

Moralism, Rationalist or Sentimental

by shift of emphasis and omission. Some things quietly disappear, others firmly embedded in liturgical tradition lose their original meaning and survive as vaguely poetic decoration.

Perhaps the easiest and most effective relation of Christian theology to the new natural science and its technology was made by the Puritans and Pietists, who made the least effort at philosophical coherence. Churches with a considerable investment in the obsolete cosmology and philosophy, such as the Roman Catholic, found it harder to come to terms with the mathematical-mechanical outlook. The great speculative systems of German Lutheran idealism revealed more of the inner world of the mind and self than the mechanistic empiricist schemes, but did not have effective connection with the expanding disciplines of natural science. The Puritans and Pietists simply compartmentalized their thought, utilizing the new manipulative knowledge of the world for practical purposes, while retaining Biblical personalist categories for the life of religion and morals. Whatever is to be said of this procedure philosophically it was surprisingly effective in practice.

There were, of course, certain areas of unavoidable conflict, which produced the familiar episodes of the "conflict of science and religion." But in public worship these cosmological novelties were less influential than the growing idealization of man and the ethical concern which shaped a strain of religious devotion parallel to that of Pietism and Evangelicalism and rivaling it. The higher man's moral capacities were estimated, the less conviction was felt about original sin, the need of redemption, or even the divinity of the Redeemer. The focus of hope tended to shift also from a fulfillment beyond time to future generations within history.

Much of the attraction of the rationalizing current grew from reaction against the sectarianism and intolerance of the rival forms of orthodoxy and Pietism. Intense convictions about the doctrines of redemption and corresponding patterns of church organization had led all Christendom into appalling civil war, in the Thirty Years' War on the Continent, and the Puritan revolution in England. Common sense and common morality now revolted against the dogmatisms of the rival theologians; they were no longer to be entrusted with the direction of governments and public affairs. They claimed to know too much and were too intolerant. The kind of Christianity needed in this ecclesiastically splintered world was commonsense religion, concentrated on the universal moral teachings and the basic common convictions of all the rival churches. In the last third of the seventeenth century such a persuasion became widespread in many quarters. There was a tacit agreement on all sides to de-emphasize the issues on which the religious wars had been fought, while maintaining a truce among the several rival traditions. Similarly there was a reaction against the belief in witches and devils and ecclesiastically sanctioned practices based on that belief.

The new religious mood and theological outlook expressed themselves both in "liturgical" and in "non-liturgical" traditions, but are somewhat easier to trace in the former case, against the more fully documented background. In the Church of England, for example, where the 1662 revision of the *Book of Common Prayer* was enforced by the police power, there is something to be learned from the various further revisions which were proposed in the next century and more.[67]

The first of two influential models for these revisions was found in the proposals of the 1689 Commission. This 1689 draft represented the last serious Anglican effort at reconciliation with the more moderate Puritans, a comprehensive platform on which one might still hope to hold together a genuinely national Church of England and avoid permanent schisms. In the 1689 proposal, the Puri-

Moralism, Rationalist or Sentimental

tan "Exceptions" of 1661 were taken with a seriousness that the bishops had withheld at the earlier date and a number of concessions were made to Puritan scruples.[68] The proposals of 1689 again failed to placate the intolerance of high church vengeance, but they remained as a platform for the irenic efforts of later decades. *The Free and Candid Disquisitions* (1749) of John Jones reprinted the 1689 reforms in an appendix and revived their influence.

Dr. Clarke's Prayer Book proposals of 1712, on the other hand, marked a stage in that process of rationalization of theology which was to move rapidly to more radical positions. Clarke was an Arian, or Semi-Arian, who declined to place Christ on a level with the Father. He did not deny the incarnation or resurrection, but balked at the Trinity. He objected to the Athanasian Creed and to any prayers directed to Christ. Of the ten or a dozen proposed Prayer Book revisions of the next two generations, the majority were unorthodox in Christology like Clarke and several showed the influence of the 1689 proposals.

Most of the new Anglican liturgies urged in the 1750's and 1760's, for example, dropped the Athanasian Creed. Several of them also dispensed with the Nicene and Apostles' Creeds as well, and the "Glory be to the Father." There were difficulties with the descent into hell, the resurrection of the body, the communion of the saints. They generally rearranged the prayers, as in the litany, so that they should be addressed only to God the Father, as was the practice in the early church. The prayer of confession was too pessimistic about man's sin for them; they wished to qualify the declaration "we have offended against thy holy laws" and to omit "there is no health in us." The absolution should be recast to make it more clear that it is not the minister who forgives sin.

On the positive side, these new liturgies sought to expand the celebration of God's creation and providential rule in hymns and responses. This was the real focus of their piety. Addison's familiar hymn voices it:

> The spacious firmament on high,
> With all the blue ethereal sky,
> And spangled heavens, a shining frame,
> Their great Original proclaim....
>
> In reason's ear they all rejoice,
> And utter forth a glorious voice;
> Forever singing, as they shine,
> "The hand that made us is divine."

They were also disposed to elaborate ethical aspiration in prayers, specifying the "relative duties" of men in their several stations in the social hierarchy. Their supplications and petitions expressed the needs of social welfare with a new concreteness (as, e.g., invoking divine protection from such disasters as the distemper of livestock).

The most influential of these rationalistic proposals was *The Book of Common Prayer Reformed According to the Plan of the Late Dr. Samuel Clarke,* which Theophilus Lindsey published in 1774 for the chapel he had founded in London as a gathering point for Anglican Unitarians. The wealthiest congregation in New England, King's Chapel in Boston, adopted Lindsey's improvements for what was to become the first Unitarian church in America. Lindsey doubtless represented a substantial current of Unitarianism within the Church of England, but few were as hopeful that the Church of England might be formally reconstituted on this basis. By the last quarter of the century, the Evangelical Awakening was beginning to gain momentum in the Church of England and it was ever less likely that the tendency represented by Lindsey would be able to reform the doctrinal and liturgical standards of the state church. After Lindsey, Unitarian movements within Anglicanism simply seceded to function as dissenting bodies if determined on liturgical reform.

Moralism, Rationalist or Sentimental

Similar tendencies, meanwhile, had made themselves felt within the "non-liturgical" traditions of dissent. Dr. Clarke won followers here also, especially among the Presbyterians. They were the wealthiest of the nonconformists and were most vulnerable to social and cultural pressure. The high attrition among those who kept carriages was noted. They had been prevailingly royalist, in contrast to the more radical Puritans, and merely desired a more comprehensive state church. As the eighteenth century wore on, they displayed conspicuously more drift to Unitarianism and leakage to Anglicanism than the other dissenters. English Presbyterianism, in fact, shrank from over half of all dissent in 1661 to almost nothing by the beginning of the nineteenth century.

As one might expect, the worship of the Presbyterians showed the change in religious attitude. The Sacraments became highly problematical and were widely omitted altogether for long periods. The traditional formula of Baptism is Trinitarian and the Lord's Supper, of course, could mean little for men who did not believe in an atonement and new life. If it were retained, it could be only as a dramatic memorial of a martyr's death. Prayer itself met with widespread disbelief and the tendency was to reduce worship simply to a lecture on topics of morality. There were hymns, to be sure, but the Arian and Socinian clergy found it expedient to expurgate and rephrase Watts and Doddridge as they did the formulae of the Sacraments. The ministerial leadership tended to move in the more radical direction across the graduated series of theological positions, Arminian, Semi-Arian, Arian, Socinian, deist. In two generations Presbyterianism in England had generally come to mean Unitarianism.

In the sphere of worship, it is interesting to note, it was the Unitarian wing that became "liturgical." Orthodox dissent, in particular the Congregationalists and Baptists, produced no spoken liturgies in this period. But a "liturgical" tendency developed in Presbyterianism in the 1750's. A Semi-Arian *Specimen of a Liturgy* was published in 1753 with an introduction vigorously attacking "free prayer." John Taylor's reply, *The Scripture Account of Prayer,* restated the prevailing view of nonconformity. There were several more Presbyterian drafts in the fifteen or twenty years after Lindsey's publication, based on his Anglican model. Over a third, in fact, of the Unitarian liturgies up to 1850 were based on Lindsey. Nearly all of the liturgical proposals of the period were Arian or Unitarian; the orthodox dissenters produced no spoken liturgies. Their creative liturgical work was in sung praise, the hymn.

The tendency of rationalistic religion to fixed liturgical forms is readily understandable. The presupposition of free prayer originally had been religious exaltation, the presence of the Spirit within saying "Abba" with our spirit. But, to the eighteenth-century moralistic Christian, whether Anglican or nonconformist, enthusiasm was "a very horrid thing." What was needed was a style of prayer in tune with the elegantly polished and eminently reasonable sermons that Tillotson had made the norm. Prayer, too, should be carefully thought out and judiciously worded beforehand. A self-consciously cultured congregation was easily offended by the solecisms and colloquialism of much free prayer.

It was a similar story across the Atlantic, except that in America the Unitarian movement developed within Congregationalism and Anglicanism rather than within Anglicanism and Presbyterianism. Up to the middle of the nineteenth century, the theologically orthodox Reformed churches in America showed no interest in liturgical forms. It was the Unitarians who produced a literature of written prayers. They remained leaders in such "liturgical" composition in the second half of the century, and into the twentieth, along with the liberal wing of Congregationalism. Through two centuries, an interest in forms of spoken prayer in the Reformed churches has been frequently associated with theological rationalism and liberalism. It had been argued[69] that the lack of a strong Eucharistic tradition is likely to lead a church into this moralizing tendency. This theory needs some qualification. The Unitarian tendency was strong in the eighteenth century in Anglicanism, Lutheranism, the Reformed churches indifferently. Its incidence seemed to reflect exposure to the dominant currents of secular culture more than any peculiarities of religious practice or ecclesiastical structure. The advantages of the churches with stronger Eucharistic and doctrinal structures lay, rather, in the stimulus they afforded to *recovery* later of the full dimensions of Christion redemption. There seem to be no institutional ways to prevent the weakening of faith, but there may be ways of facilitating renewal. In the early nineteenth century the Reformed churches seemed often slower to recover than the Lutheran or Anglican or Roman Catholic. And here the greater disintegration of a Eucharistic practice may have been a significant factor.

Some of the Continental Reformed churches exhibited in less acute form the divergent tendencies that had led to actual schism between Episcopalianism and the free churches in England. In France and French Switzerland, for example, there was a marked contrast in the eighteenth century between the well-to-do upper-class urban Huguenots, who pinned their hopes to royal indulgence, and the popular churches of the Camisard resistance, fighting fiercely for ecclesiastical self-government. The former admired the royal patronage, episcopal government, and Prayer Book worship of Anglicanism, and it was among them that one found a tendency to theological rationalism clothed in elegant language. The persecuted communities of the French Reformed, on the other hand, sought to retain their traditional worship and doctrine unchanged. Much of it was necessarily underground and much without the leadership of ordained ministers. Lay readers and precentors would call the church together and lead in worship. The prayers and Scripture would be read and sometimes written sermons. Psalms were sung when it was considered safe. By the mid-eighteenth century, the old prohibition against lining out psalms was relaxed. Pulpits and Communion tables were sometimes made ingeniously of several parts entrusted separately to different families, so that they could be assembled for actual use and then hidden separately. The subsidence of persecution in the last third of the century freed the French church to consider changes in worship. The chief models before them then were the new liturgies of French Switzerland.

French Switzerland had maintained the Reformation tradition through the seventeenth century, but, at the beginning of the eighteenth, a new generation of churchmen appeared who led the church into new theological paths. Their leaders were J. A. Turretin and B. Pictet of Geneva and J. F. Osterwald of Neuchâtel. They were in correspondence with some Anglicans, such as Wake, and shared the latitudinarian tendencies prevalent in the Church of England. They attempted to reshape the Calvinist liturgies more to the model of the *Book of Common Prayer* and to voice Arminian or Semi-Arian theology.

Turretin and Pictet were assigned to propose revisions for the Genevan liturgy in 1703, but, before their work was complete, Osterwald's theological orientation was already evident in his catechism of 1704, from which he omitted original sin and predestination. In Eucharistic doctrine he held a merely memorialist view. Justification by faith also underwent a sea change in his exposition. In the interest of these theological convictions he composed in 1706 a new liturgy on the model of the Anglican *Book of Common Prayer*. The preface of the 1713 publication was a manifesto of liturgical reform. The reform might be described as an "enrichment" of non-Eucharistic worship with ancient elements, at the expense of preaching and free prayer.

Osterwald considered the Calvinist liturgy "terribly disfigured," "dry," and "cold," and wished to introduce more unction. But he did not trust free ("arbitrary") prayer and eliminated it from the service. A series of short collects with congregational "Amens" seemed to him better calculated to hold the attention of the congregation than the long prayers of the older liturgy. He expressed interest in the antiphons of the ancient church in his preface, but did not dare propose congregational responses.

Sermons had been overemphasized, in Osterwald's judgment, and for his weekday morning and evening services for Mondays, Thursdays, and Saturdays no sermons were scheduled. Instead he wished to stress the simple reading of Scripture as an act of worship. The old custom of a separate reader's service before the main service had lowered the dignity of Scripture-reading and most people did not attend the reader's service at all. Osterwald would have liked to get the reading of Scripture back into the main Lord's Day service, but was unsuccessful. He had to begin his rehabilitation of Scripture-reading in the weekday services. This liturgical reading of Scripture was his most controversial proposal. To be sure, Osterwald supplied a set of "reflections" on the Scripture lessons which were to be read as printed.

Besides these general conceptions, Osterwald admired some of the patristic forms preserved in the Anglican *Book of Common Prayer*. He recovered the ancient dialogue form of the preface to the Eucharistic prayer from the "Lift up your hearts" through the "Holy, holy, holy." But it was clear from his doctrine of the Eucharist that this formula was actually intended to mean less than the current Calvinist usage. Similarly, the Kyrie Eleison and the "Glory be to God on high" appeared in his liturgy, and New Testament canticles along with the psalms. But he did not use either the Nicene or Athanasian Creeds and cut down on the use of the Apostles' Creed. There was here no such Eucharistic emphasis as in the Reformation. For Osterwald, the Sacraments were "sacred ceremonies" performed out of obedience. Confirmation was more important than Baptism.

Of the half dozen congregations of Huguenot refugees in colonial South Carolina, that of Charleston adopted the Neuchâtel liturgy. This congregation was a reestablishment of that of Pons, where the church building was destroyed in the persecution of 1687. The other five refugee French churches in Carolina were forced to conform to the Anglican state church, but Charleston continued its French liturgy, publishing an English translation of it in 1853.

Osterwald's ideas were influential also in Geneva, in Vaud, and in France. In Geneva the revisions were debated for decades, and the new liturgy of Turretin did not finally appear until 1723. Here also Anglican and Lutheran models were emulated and the free prayer before and after the sermon was eliminated. Here also depravity and original sin were toned down in the prayer of confession. The new birth became "a great change in us." Instead of a sacrament, one found a "ceremony which represents the great change which ought to occur." Even so the changes in sermons and hymns were more extensive than those of the liturgy. One recalls Rousseau's contemptuous reference to the "shame-faced Socinians" in the pulpits of Geneva. By the early nineteenth century, this description was generally apt. Geneva and Massachusetts Bay, two of the most famous nurseries of the Reformed Church, had, by that time, both largely collapsed into Unitarianism. In the process, they had grown more "liturgical" in the sense of using more set forms.

In the last generation of the eighteenth century the Reformed Church in France finally enjoyed religious liberty

Moralism, Rationalist or Sentimental 145

and public security. At least some of the Swiss innovations were adopted. New Testament canticles were utilized along with the psalms and a system of Scripture readings. But when the Geneva ministers produced a Unitarian version of the Bible, the French Reformed refused to use it. They were, of course, preoccupied from the 1790's with the catastrophic political changes.

In Germany the Reformed had suffered terribly, as in France and Hungary, from the militant Counter-Reformation. Not only did the Reformed districts of Germany bear the worst of the Thirty Years' War, but a generation later the beautiful Rhine Palatinate, the center of Reformed strength, was ravaged and rendered as uninhabitable as Louis XIV could make it. Palatine refugees moved in various directions, founding, among other things, the German Reformed Church in North America. At the same time, tens of thousands of French Reformed victims of the Sun King were establishing Reformed congregations here and there in Germany, as in Holland, England, and America. The German Reformed lost their schools and universities and were broken into fragments. Through the eighteenth century a succession of Roman Catholic princes oppressed them in various ways.

The moralistic current in religion made itself felt more and sooner among German Lutherans than among the Reformed. The progress of the tendency can be traced by the successive revised editions of liturgies, hymnals, catechetical manuals. Perhaps the most notable individual figure was Zollikofer, the famous preacher, who, although Swiss in origin, was for thirty years one of the notable figures in overwhelmingly Lutheran Leipzig. Zollikofer's *Neues Gesangbuch* of 1766 was one of the earliest reforming efforts. It contained over four hundred hymns and only twenty-seven psalms. A second edition was needed the next year. The pattern was followed in later decades in the Palatinate (1785) and Basel (1809) so that, by the early nineteenth century, little was left of the old metrical psalms and the hymns were largely of rationalistic coloring. There were also some new versions of the psalms. Gellert's hymns were found often in these Reformed hymnals as well as in the Lutheran.

Zollikofer also published one of the earliest notable revisions of the liturgy with his *Anreden und Gebete* (1777). Others, such as Hermes and Seiler, followed in the 1780's. Zollikofer's liturgy utilized in part the deist order of the Englishman David Williams (1776). Characteristic was the creed which Zollikofer substituted for the Apostles' Creed, with its extended treatment of God's attributes and providential rule, and of man's duties, with nothing said of redemption. Zollikofer also recast the Communion service in the same spirit.

The hymnals of Mieg and Pauli were more definitely and systematically rationalist than Zollikofer's. Pauli also published a version of the Heidelberg Catechism with the polemic references omitted and the hard sayings in small type.

The union with the Lutherans in the early nineteenth century assimilated many of the German Reformed to the Lutheran tradition in worship. In various localities, and sometimes under political pressure, Lutheran usages had already been taken up by Reformed groups. Thus, the liturgy of Hesse-Cassel of 1657, e.g., adopted a lectionary in place of the more general Reformed custom of preaching in course through whole books of the Bible. Bremen had done likewise, and had used hymns and practiced weekly Communion under Lutheran influence. This tendency became very widespread in the first generation of the nineteenth century when the merger movement was taken up so widely by German governments, and even by the Dutch in their colonies. In many cases, it meant the removal of Communion tables for casket altars, sometimes with candles, crucifixes, wafers for Communion. But this

Moralism, Rationalist or Sentimental

nineteenth-century development was affected by the romantic movement in all communions to which we must turn in our next chapter.

Moralism and rationalism were probably stronger in the Dutch than in either the French or German Reformed communities in the eighteenth and early nineteenth centuries. Pietism remained a living tradition among the people, but the educated classes and magistrates were much influenced by Voltaire and Rousseau, Price and Priestley. When Wolff had lost his post in Prussia, the University of Utrecht offered him refuge. All this meant a widespread questioning of original sin, election, justification by grace, miracles, and Biblical inspiration. Catechetical preaching was neglected and the afternoon service was often discontinued altogether, as Sabbath observance decreased. So far as liturgical forms are concerned, the issue was focused most sharply with the questions required in the form for infant Baptism, which were debated in several centers.

The French invasion of 1793 brought disestablishment of the Reformed Church and religious liberty. For a time the use of church bells and ministerial dress were banned and the Sabbath laws revoked. Then in the Restoration after Napoleon the synods endeavored to require catechetical preaching again, to legislate against private Baptism, and to provide a new form of congregational interrogation in the service preparatory for the Lord's Supper.

The most explosive issue turned out to be the official authorization of hymns by the Synod of 1807. Conservatives who maintained the exclusive prerogative of psalms, as laid down at Dort, fought bitterly. The issue was significant in the schism of Scholte and de Cock in 1834, which eventuated in the migrations to Iowa and Michigan led by Scholte and Van Raalte, and the founding of the Midwestern half of the Dutch Reformed Church in the United States.

A manifestation of the rationalist tendency of a somewhat different type may be noted on the American frontier in the second quarter of the nineteenth century. This was the rise of the Disciples of Christ, the only substantial new Protestant denomination indigenous to the United States.

The Disciples arose in the context of the Second Great Awakening on the frontier, and in some measure as a protest against revivalism. The most influential leaders, Thomas and Alexander Campbell and Barton Stone, were of Presbyterian extraction, but there were comparable tendencies among Methodists and Congregationalists. The Campbells were in reaction against the narrow sectarianism of the antiburgher seceder splinter of Ulster Presbyterianism, and Stone against the preaching of reprobation. All were seeking a new basis for Christian community on the frontier, where the vestiges of denominational loyalties held apart the people who should be cooperating in establishing an effective Christian nucleus. With the weapon of Lockean rationalism the attempt was made to dissolve all divisive ecclesiastical traditions in order to unite on the simple platform of the New Testament. "Where the Bible speaks, we speak; where the Bible is silent, we are silent."

It was a program of rationalizing simplification on the basis of a naïve laic Biblicism in the interest of church unity. The practices in worship seem to have been influenced by the Scottish followers of Glas and Sandeman. In contrast to the austerities of the rare Presbyterian Communion seasons, a brief memorialist Communion served by elders and deacons and stressing fellowship and joy was made central in every service. This came first, whether or not preaching followed, and evidently held together many congregations unable to secure a preacher. Baptism must be by immersion, on the New Testament model, and as such was a necessary qualification for Communion. Both Sacraments were viewed as ordinances enjoined by Scripture, rather legalistically, and with no mystical or enthusiastic sense. Faith, likewise, was a matter of assent to prescribed teachings, rather than primarily trust, as with the Reformers. Christianity was presented as a clear-cut formula for salvation, to be accepted and obeyed, without revivalist emotionalism or appeals to the grace of the Holy Spirit. With all the striking differences in social situation and cultural level there were here visible some of the dominant motives of latitudinarian Anglicanism.

Other instances of a moralistic and rationalistic type of religion in the Reformed churches might be found in the history of the nineteenth and twentieth centuries. Much of the literary, musical, and architectural "enrichment" of worship in American liberal Protestantism has had this character. Monumental buildings imitating European cathedrals, elaborate organs and carillons, professional soloists and choirs, and prayers in archaic cadence have often been utilized to demonstrate the financial resources and cultural pretensions of congregations whose faith was primarily moralism. Often the lack of seriousness is betrayed by the combination of symbols of disparate theological meanings.

The initiative for "enrichment" often came from the Sunday school, where various devices were studied to develop a mood of devotion. An altar provided a "visual focus," and the ceremonial lighting and extinguishing of candles added to the interest if not to illumination. Processions in colored surplices, responses sung through half-closed doors, even religious dance helped to disguise the erosion of theological substance.

After the Second World War, for example, the American Congregationalists produced a *Book of Worship for Free Churches*.[70] The introduction set forth two alternative arrangements for the Lord's Supper as equally suitable. One was the familiar Congregational Holy Table. The other was a full kit of Roman or Anglo-Catholic paraphernalia, with a casket altar against the east wall in a "sanctuary" reserved for the clergy alone. There was advice about the mensa, credence table, reredos, superfrontal, retable, the three white cloths without lace or tassels, surplice and stole, the five "liturgical" colors for the several seasons and a table of fixed holy days, including Saint Michael and All Angels, Saint Simon and Saint Jude, Saint Mathias, along with Rural Life Sunday (liturgical color: white), Thanksgiving, and Reformation Sunday (both, apparently, liturgically "green").

The "Lift up your hearts" sequence from the Eucharistic prayer was torn from context to become a "Call to prayer," followed by the "Glory be to the Father," and the "Holy, holy, holy" appeared as a choral response to the Scripture-reading. "Symbolism" was everywhere. "For the word of God there is the open Bible and some would also add the flowers suggesting the creative power of his word.... Numbers also have significance: one is for God, two for the two natures of Christ in the Incarnation, three for the Trinity, four for the four Gospels or for the wide earth, five for the five wounds of Christ, six for imperfections, seven for perfection, eight for regeneration and the beginning of man's life after the seven days of creation.... The narthex and nave may be said to typify the world, and the chancel, heaven. The center aisle represents the march of life, from birth to entrance into eternity, the baptismal font being anciently at the entrance end and the altar at the far end of the aisle."

But, if one studies the Communion service to be performed in this pseudo-Catholic setting, on this casket altar without relics by a priest without "orders," the real meaning becomes clear. In the preparatory section use is made of the prayer of general confession from the Anglican matins. But, whereas the Puritan ancestors had found this prayer disappointingly vague on original sin, their successors now found it necessary even to delete the phrases "miserable offenders," and "no health in us." The service is

Moralism, Rationalist or Sentimental 151

essentially "Zwinglian," if not Unitarian, a memorial of the martyrdom of Jesus and a dedication to his service. There is no genuine sacramental concern here. Similarly the baptismal service is simply a dedication of the child.

The incongruities occasioned by the inconsiderate use of religious symbolism, however, should not blind us to the real services of religious moralism and rationalism. Again and again it has been needed to liberate deeper forms of Christianity, Protestant and Catholic alike, from obscurantism, idolatry, sectarianism, and intolerance. There are, for example, serious problems of conscience for many in the liturgical use of the Catholic creeds, problems that are not solved by the sophisticated interpretations of the theologians. The health of the church has often been served by the Unitarian demand for intellectual integrity.

From the seventeenth century to the present day this has been the actual working religion of an important body of laymen in all the traditions of Western Christendom. It has represented a sincere faith in the Creator and Judge of men, and an endeavor to honor him in public life. In this respect it has continued the characteristic Reformed stress on the relation of worship to vocation better than some of the Evangelicals and Pietists.

VIII
CATHOLIC TRADITIONALISM

Past the middle of the nineteenth century the worship of the Reformed churches of the world conformed generally to one or both of two patterns in worship, that of the Evangelicals, on the one hand, and on the other, that of the Moderates, to use the party labels of Scotland. This was primarily a preaching tradition in either case, although the celebrations of the Lord's Supper, infrequent as they were, were taken with great seriousness. The two tendencies differed more in tone and theological meaning than in form, although the moralistic camp was ready at times to use set liturgical forms.

This familiar configuration was reoriented and complicated, however, by the injection of a new third alternative in the middle of the nineteenth century, an alternative that has been increasingly influential ever since. This alternative is the adaptation of historical Catholic conceptions and forms of worship, especially of Eucharistic worship. These forms and conceptions established themselves in a few Reformed centers in the day of cultural romanticism and political reaction. From these beachheads they have increasingly penetrated the main Reformed bodies, although to the present day this third tendency is far less influential than the other two. The legacy of anti-Romanism has been a formidable obstacle, succeeding as it has, e.g., at one time and place or another, in banning the congregational use of the Lord's Prayer, the celebration of Christmas, the singing of hymns, the wearing of Geneva gowns. The Catholicizing tendency, however, has at least established its right to existence in these churches and won official toleration.

The motives and purposes of the modern Catholicizing tendency have not remained the same through the three or more generations of its life. They have varied with the uses of history in general, for a Catholicizing tendency by definition represents a distinctive attitude to history, a special kind of historical consciousness. In the first two generations, the movement was largely dominated by traditionalism, by the nostalgic attempt to repristinate ancient attitudes and forms as a strategy of institutional defense. It was in considerable measure a reaction against the rationalization of life in an increasingly commercial and industrial society, a celebration of the mysterious, numinous, and supernatural in a matter-of-fact bourgeois world. It was also antidemocratic and clerical, cultivating in ecclesiastical setting and for the clergy the triumphalist insignia of empire and courts, of earthly power and its trappings, from a day when priests commanded the temporal as well as the spiritual sword. In the twentieth century, however, Catholicism can no longer be simply identified with medievalism. The triumphalist and archaizing motifs have receded while the missionary and pastoral concerns are more determinative. The modern ecumenical movement is inconceivable without that new kind of historical consciousness which transcends traditionalist romanticism.

Throughout the nineteenth century and the first part of the twentieth, the Anglican *Book of Common Prayer* was the most influential channel of traditional forms, at least in the English-speaking world. Lutheranism, with all its rich liturgical heritage, was a much larger body in the United States than the Protestant Episcopal community, but the *Book of Common Prayer* remained in the English-speaking world generally *the* representative model of a "Catholic" liturgical tradition.

Most of the widespread borrowing from the Prayer Book, to be sure, represented a merely literary and aesthetic admiration, rather than a religious or theological persuasion. (One might perhaps make the same assessment of Anglican feelings about the book.) The prayer of general confession, the general thanksgiving, Cranmer's version of the "Lift up your hearts" turned up in services of congregations of various denominations with some frequency in the nineteenth century. Less often one heard the prose psalms chanted, a collect, or festival prayer. The Anglican version of the church calendar was also influential and the marriage service most of all. But none of this had any necessary or even usual association with high sacramental views or a high doctrine of the church, which are the marks of a genuine Catholic inclination.

In addition to the exploitation of Anglican traditionalism by other Protestant bodies, the church historians rediscovered the other liturgies of the Reformation. Most Reformed churches of the mid-nineteenth century had been so long dominated by the effects of Puritan and Pietist hostility to liturgical forms that they were no longer aware of their own liturgical heritage. Many were shocked by the publications of the texts in the 1840's and 1850's, of the liturgies of Calvin's Geneva (1849) and Knox's Scotland (1840), of the Reformed Church of the Palatinate (1855), of the Charleston version of the Neuchâtel liturgy (1853), of the treasury of prayers in J. H. A. Ebrard's *Kirchenbuch* (1846) and C. W. Baird's *Book of Prayers* (1857), and most comprehensively, by the general account of Reformed worship in Baird's *Eutaxia: or the Presbyterian Liturgies. Historical Sketches* (1855). Presbyterian liturgies indeed! It sounded a century ago like a contradiction in terms.

But the historical case, however surprising to many, was unassailable. And most of the editors of these various liturgical texts presented them not just as historical curiosities but as models, or at least suggestions, for practical use. There was evidently a desire within the Reformed churches of several countries for more formal worship in conscious continuity with that of generations past. Some revival of Reformation conceptions of the church and sacraments also became a live possibility, although most Reformed peoples had no sense of how far they had drifted from the Reformation in these matters.

In fact, however, very few of the sixteenth-century spoken prayers commended themselves for actual use in the second half of the nineteenth century. They were too didactic and too prickly with polemic, and on issues that were no longer urgent. They were full of references to circumstances that had become obscure and irrelevant. The only sixteenth-century Reformed liturgy still in even partial use, unless one included the Anglican *Book of Common Prayer,* was that of the Dutch Reformed, and that clearly needed revision. Individual prayers were still usable, and basic structures, but no liturgy as a whole. The best-loved and most influential elements of the old liturgies, the metrical psalms, were so archaic as to disenchant all but the most determined Reformed traditionalists.

The attempt to revive Reformation orders of service was thus abortive. But the effort was important as dramatizing the fact that the Reformed churches had originally used liturgical forms. And if sixteenth-century forms were no longer satisfactory as they stood, could one go behind them? After all, the Reformers had conceived themselves as Reformed *Catholics* and had appealed in some measure to patristic precedents in matters of worship as well as discipline and theology. Might there not be forms of service in the legacy of pre-Reformation Catholicism which the Reformers had not appropriated but which were compatible with Reformed theology and suitable for modern churches, wishing to affirm historical continuity?

The first significant Catholicizing movements in the Reformed context did not, however, present themselves in such ingratiating and diplomatic guise. It is perhaps indicative of the abyss between the nineteenth-century Reformed churches and "Catholicism" generally that the two movements which initiated the Catholic tendency in these churches explicitly repudiated their Reformed historical origin.

The first was the Catholic Apostolic Church, which denied the full legitimacy of all existing ecclesiastical bodies and proclaimed a new Pentecost and a new apostolate as harbingers of the Lord's imminent return. The second was the Anglo-Catholic movement, which repudiated the Protestant character of Anglicanism and attempted to assimilate it partly to patristic models but more to medieval and Counter-Reformation Roman Catholicism. The Evangelical Catholic movement in the American German Reformed Church, finally, was the first to try to relate itself responsibly both to ancient Catholicism and to the Reformation. All three movements were churchly, laid new weight on the Real Presence in the Eucharist, on baptismal grace, and made new claims for the authority of the ministry.

The Catholic Apostolic Church grew out of High Church Scottish Presbyterianism caught up in eschatological enthusiasm and the gift of Pentecostal "tongues." First gathered around the preaching of Edward Irving, the congregation passed after his death (1834) into the hands of a new dispensation of Apostles appointed by the Holy Spirit. Under the Apostles John B. Cardale and Henry Drummond the charismatic spontaneity of the Spirit was rapidly channeled into a highly hierarchical and authoritarian institution with elaborate liturgy and ritual. Their service book was first published in 1842 as *The Liturgy and Other Divine Offices of the Church,* but a weekly

Eucharist had been their central service for half a dozen years. Later editions, in 1847 and 1850, were progressively more elaborate, acquiring medieval vestments, incense, lights, holy water, reservation of the elements.

The liturgy was apparently chiefly Cardale's work and is to be interpreted especially by his *Readings on the Liturgy* (1852). It reveals a rather impressive level of liturgical scholarship, especially in Greek and patristic materials. Cardale exploited the classical liturgical studies of the seventeenth-century Roman Catholic pioneers, e.g., the Dominican Goar's Greek texts from *Euchologion* (1667), the *Thesaurus sacrorum rituum* of the Barnabite Bartolomeus Gavantus, in Merati's eighteenth-century edition (1736–1738), and Cardinal Bona's *Rerum liturgicarum libri duo* (1671), the first comprehensive history of the Mass. For Western texts and usages, especially Gallican, he had the four volumes of the Maurist Dom Martène, *De antiquis ecclesiae ritibus editio secunda* (1735–1738). These and other similar works put at his disposal a wealth of historical material unknown to the Reformers or the Counter-Reformation. Cardale handled it with considerable independence, nerved no doubt by his sense of Apostolic responsibility, shaping a service book with coherence and character. Friedrich Heiler described it enthusiastically as "undoubtedly one of the finest and fullest forms of Christian worship. Indeed, of all the liturgies of today it comes perhaps nearest the Primitive church."[71]

Transubstantiation was denied, but the Real Presence was conceived as localized in the consecrated elements, which were reserved and used throughout the week at the obligatory daily offices. All worship was thus Eucharistic, or more accurately, related to the local Presence. The various areas of the church building were more or less sacred in ratio to their proximity to the altar and its tabernacle, a conception more baroque than patristic or medieval. Ceremonial, lights, medieval vestments, washings, all articulated this conception of a localized Presence. The bloodless "sacrifice" of the consecrated elements was interpreted as fulfillment and "antitype" of the various forms of Old Testament sacrifice, burnt offering, peace offering, sin offering. An ecclesiastical yearly cycle was followed, something between the Orthodox and the Roman. Collects and anthems were varied, not by the week, as with the Latin church, but much less frequently, by the "seasons," as of the Nativity, the Resurrection, and Pentecost. There was a fourfold hierarchy of the charismatic ministry, Apostles, Prophets, Evangelists, Pastors, and in local churches there were Angels, Elders, and Deacons. Preaching at the weekly Eucharistic service was restricted to ten minutes and carefully censored. The whole of this worship was pervaded by the characteristic mood of expectancy and anticipation of the Lord's imminent Return. Few types of modern worship have so vividly reproduced the eschatological orientation of the church of the apostles.

The Catholic Apostolic Church embodied the conviction that there had been no perfectly catholic and apostolic church on earth since the original apostles, and began church history, so to speak, all over again in eschatological urgency. The Anglo-Catholic movement, our second instance, was equally negative as regards Protestantism, but idealized Catholicism in its pre-Reformation form, and in considerable degree in its modern Counter-Reformation phase. Anglo-Catholicism yearned back to the preindustrial and predemocratic days when knighthood was in flower and priests were arrogant. It might itself be described not too unfairly as the Counter-Reformation in Anglicanism, eventuating in a kind of inverted Uniate pattern, assimilated to Roman Catholicism in everything *but* clerical discipline and papal obedience. It was only a party, of course, and not a church, and remained in a strained posture of continual polemic and insubordination to the bishops.

Catholic Traditionalism

The contributions of this movement were not literary, as with the Catholic Apostolic liturgy. The Ritualists were nominally bound to the *Book of Common Prayer* and in no position to produce major revisions of liturgical texts like the Irvingites. They did develop some scholars of liturgical history such as J. M. Neale, W. Palmer, W. Maskell, W. Bright. And there was considerable surreptitious doctoring of the *Book of Common Prayer* in practice by way of assimilation to the Tridentine Mass.

But the distinctive contribution of the Anglo-Catholic Ritualists was not in liturgical texts, but in the sphere of ceremonial, architecture, and the apparatus of worship. The theological innovations of the Oxford *Tracts* and the writings of Wilberforce, in particular, became identified in a few years with a series of ceremonial usages worn as badges of party. As once the Puritans had stumbled at kneeling reception of Communion, the sign of the cross in Baptism, the ring in marriage, so now the Ritualists invited martyrdom for the "eastward position," the mixed chalice, wafer bread, medieval vestments, kneelings and prostratings.

One is reminded of the tactics of such men as Bishop Gardiner in the Reformation to read definitely Roman meanings into the 1549 *Book of Common Prayer* by means of ceremonial. Altar lights, incense, kneeling, and adoration of the consecrated elements were employed to indicate a localized presence; medieval Mass vestments testified to a propitiatory cultic action. These practices had not been enjoined by the founders. Newman and Pusey were "north-enders" and never used chasubles, incense, lights, or crosses. Newman served Communion in the pews at St. Mary's. Pusey later counseled against imposing Romanizing innovations without the understanding or consent of congregations. But such tyrannizing over the consciences of the laity was widely practiced in the ritualist wars which dominated the second half of the century in the Church of

England. There were scandalous riots, protest meetings, disciplinary actions, prosecutions, and actual imprisonments until at length discipline was effectively broken down. And by the twentieth century Anglicanism had learned to tolerate most of these innovations. It has remained also probably the most self-conscious church in Christendom in ceremonial matters.

Perhaps the most widely influential Anglo-Catholic innovations were in the spheres of architectural appointments and music. J. M. Neale, with his Cambridge Camden Society and his Ecclesiological Society, carried on from the 1840's an astonishingly successful propaganda for a "Catholic" church architecture. There was, it appeared, only one truly "Christian style" for a church, even though Christianity had managed to get along for over a thousand years before it had been invented. This was the Gothic of the fourteenth century, a period now discovered, somewhat curiously, to have been the great "age of faith." It was the mark of a "church," as against a mere "conventicle," to have pointed arches, transepts, and a chancel for at least a third of the interior length. The altar, however, was to be placed on a raised platform and visible at all times, indicating a baroque and theatrical Counter-Reformation conception rather than a truly Gothic one.

Such appointments, which were prescribed in minute detail by the "ecclesiologists," were rationalized in terms of spurious allegory after the style of Durandus. The cruciform ground plan, e.g., was postulated as an allegory of the atoning passion. The font was moved away from the forepart of the building and put by the door as an allegory of the entrance into the Christian life. The tripartite division of nave and side aisles represented the Holy Trinity. The rood screen symbolized the passage by death from the church militant (nave) to the church triumphant (sanctuary). Even Archbishop Laud had referred to Durandus' theories as "delirium." He should have lived to browse

Catholic Traditionalism

through the shelves of ritualist "symbolism" and "religious art."

The huge empty "Gothic" chancels could not be made to seem occupied, even with all the proliferation of eagle lecterns, stone altars, litany desks, kneeling stools, and the solemn parading back and forth from one to the other by the clergyman. The principle "no chancel no church" would hardly have been made good had it not coincided with a new development in church music. This was the advocacy of cathedral choral music for all congregations and so far as possible for all services, as advocated especially by John Jebb. Jebb explicitly opposed congregational singing as a "mistaken and modern notion."[72] Congregations should sit and hear the professionals do it correctly. The proposal was now made that choirs should be put in surplices and seated in those long, empty chancels between congregation and altar. The choir thus replaced the medieval clerical chapter in the cathedral, and even a parish church with a vicar could with this staff of chanting surpliced laymen seem like a cathedral. The choir was moved down from the rear loft, where it had served to support congregational participation, into the chancel where it was to perform the service with the clergy instead and on behalf of the congregation. Plainsong was revived, and clergymen increasingly intoned services, both morning prayer and the Communion service.

The first church of note arranged on this pattern was that of Leeds in the 1840's, but it has in the century or so since become very familiar all over the English-speaking world. Not all the congregations that have adopted it have intended, like its inventors, to suppress congregational participation, but the logic of the arrangement has made itself felt. Even in churches with no tendency to sacerdotalism, the use of robed choirs in chancels tends to approximate the worship service to a concert of sacred music, and works against congregational worship. Perhaps the most unfortunate legacy of the Anglo-Catholic movement to the Reformed churches generally has been this epidemic of chancels and theatrical choirs.

The most constructive contribution, ironically, is a notable addition to the repertory of hymns for congregational use. The greatest single hymn writer of the movement was J. M. Neale. Most of Neale's ministry was passed as chaplain in a home for the elderly, where he could perform the Mass in Latin in a chasuble, invoke the intercession of the Virgin, use the Roman breviary, hear confessions, and editorialize about the "Catholic" correctness of church buildings all over England while defying his bishop's regulations as "totally invalid." Neale had scorned the Protestant hymnody of Watts and Wesley as irreverent and vulgar, if not heretical, and opposed the whole idea until he discovered that the early church had practiced it. With this authorization his "fatal facility for versifying," as he called it, was unleashed and made him the most prolific Anglo-Catholic hymn writer, earning a ranking of third or fourth in most Presbyterian and Methodist hymnals of the twentieth century, right after Wesley and Watts. We owe to this obsessed anti-Protestant such hymns as "Of the Father's Love Begotten," "All Glory, Laud, and Honor," "Jerusalem the Golden," "O Come, O Come, Emmanuel," "Good Christian Men, Rejoice," "The Day of Resurrection!" "Come, Ye Faithful, Raise the Strain," "Christ Is Made the Sure Foundation." Neale translated, usually rather freely, many Greek and Latin hymns, strengthening thus an awareness of ancient tradition and the continuity of the church. The hymns were far more influential than the liturgical texts he published.

Such in outline were the two "Catholic" movements that challenged the Reformed churches in the middle generation of the last century. The immediate reaction was overwhelmingly and emphatically hostile. But in time it was conceded that their influence had made for greater dignity and reverence in public worship, and especially for increased Eucharistic worship. The Reformed churches generally left room for improvement in these directions, even while unlikely to adopt the antiquarian obscurantism, the clericalism, the medieval individualism with which they had been associated by the "Catholic" movements. The ideological coloring of both movements, their reactionary Toryism, was qualified in time. Ritualist priests, exiled to undesirable parishes in the slums, discovered unexpected evangelistic uses with subliterate people for dramatic ceremonial practices they had championed for other reasons. Cassocks and sandals, an aristocratic antiquarian affectation in the mother country, appeared on missionaries in India or Africa as less alien and affected than the modern European garb of Protestant missionaries. And Anglo-Catholicism, at least, acquired in the second generation from the broad churchmen an admirable ethical passion.

The first notable effort to assimilate some of this Catholicizing effort within an explicitly Reformed context was, as noted, the Evangelical Catholic movement within the German Reformed Church of the United States. Unlike both Anglo-Catholic and Catholic Apostolic parties, the Evangelical Catholics affirmed *both* their Reformation heritage and that of ancient Catholicism, and wrestled with the ecumenical task implicit in that recognition. They claimed to be genuine Catholics genuinely reformed, and shaped a liturgy[73] (1857 first edition, 1866 second edition) to express that claim.

Nevin's *Mystical Presence* (1847) measured the current Eucharistic teachings and practices of American Protestantism, Lutheran, Episcopalian, and Reformed alike, against the teachings of the Reformed confessions and Calvin and found them all predominantly "Zwinglian." Most American Protestants were not even aware of what the Reformation position was. Nevin urged a recovery of the high Calvinist view of church and Sacraments, claiming that these were a legitimate "development" of patristic as well as Biblical teachings, and attempted a theological restatement in the idealist and "organismic" categories of the nineteenth century. He drove home the fact that nineteenth-century Protestantism, even in its more self-consciously orthodox varieties, was in fact occupying a quite different position from that of the Reformers and the confessions on matters of church, ministry, and Sacraments.

Philip Schaff presided over the liturgical commission and brought to it the fruit of the extensive debate and historical research that had been occasioned in Germany by the attempt of the King of Prussia to impose his liturgy in the United Church at the beginning of the 1820's. The remit to the commission read:

> The liturgical worship of the Primitive Church, as far as it can be ascertained from the Holy Scriptures, the oldest ecclesiastical writers, and the liturgies of the Greek and Latin Churches of the third and fourth centuries, ought to be made, as much as possible, the *general base* of the proposed Liturgy; the more so, as they are in fact also the source from which the best portions of the various Liturgies of the sixteenth century were derived.[74]

After several tries, the Communion service of the new liturgy was finally stabilized on the model of that of the Catholic Apostolic Church. Schaff had attended such a service in London in 1854 and found it "the most beautiful and perfect liturgical service I have yet attended."[75] The Eucharistic prayer exhibited the patristic pattern with the opening dialogue form of the "Lift up your hearts" through the thanksgiving and "Holy, holy, holy," the epiclesis or prayer of invocation on the bread and wine and the memorial of Christ's redemptive work as representation of his perpetual sacrifice and intercession. As in the *Book of Common Prayer* the worship of the congregation

Catholic Traditionalism

and its self-dedication as sacrifice was conjoined to the atoning sacrifice of Christ memorialized in the action. The use of an "altar" instead of the table emphasized the idea of cultic sacrifice. This conflation of two very different meanings of "sacrifice" had been traditionally regarded as misleading and unwise in the Reformed churches generally.

The German Reformed treatment of the church calendar was less like that of the Catholic Apostolic Church than the *Book of Common Prayer*. The chief festivals of Christmas, Epiphany, Good Friday, Easter, Ascension, Pentecost, Trinity, were restored as in the sixteenth-century practice of the Reformed churches (other than Scotland). Festival prayers and Scripture readings were supplied for all of these. But beyond this the committee supplied readings and collects for all the other Sundays, thus quite abandoning the older German Reformed system of continuous reading and expository preaching. (This system had already been broken down by Puritan and Pietist preaching.) The committee found many of the *Book of Common Prayer* collects, like those of the Mass, to be only loosely related, if at all, to the readings, and supplied new ones. The Communion service was intended to be the governing one, but since the most the committee felt able to enjoin was "at least twice a year, and if possible, oftener," the preaching service was in fact the normal one.

This service book found very little use as intended, as a people's book. It was bitterly opposed as Romanizing and was finally accepted only as an optional order. Even then its chief use was as a pulpit manual at the discretion of ministers. As such it was widely distributed, as much outside the denomination as within, and had considerable diffused influence. It was a landmark when a Reformed church authorized such a service book even for voluntary use.

No other Reformed church was to make such authorization until the end of the nineteenth century save the Dutch Reformed in America, who, as we have noted, had maintained throughout partial use of their Reformation service. Through the last third of the century, however, there was clearly an expanding market among Reformed ministers for manuals of public worship, and a score or more of private service books of some significance appeared, chiefly in Great Britain and the United States, but also in France.[76] Then, beginning with the English Presbyterians in 1898, one after another of the Presbyterian and Congregationalist denominations of England, Scotland, South Africa, Canada, and the United States authorized denominational volumes, joined by the Methodists and the United Church of Canada. These denominational authorizations really do not mean very much more than the private publications, since they signified only that ministers so inclined had denominational license to use the book. The committees that produced them represented minorities, as did the congregations that used them systematically. Even bare toleration was not always granted easily. A determined and bitter fight was staged in 1905, e.g., in the Presbyterian Church in the U.S.A., to prevent denominational authorization of what came to be its *Book of Common Worship*. This broadening toleration for the use of set forms of prayer, accompanied as it often was by controversy, is reminiscent of the struggle of the eighteenth and early nineteenth centuries to admit hymns beside the psalms for public praise. In each case the new patterns began with individuals and with smaller church bodies and finally established themselves in the larger denominations. And the practice of using a prayer book in and of itself indicates nothing as to theological intent, Reformed, "Catholic," or otherwise, as is sufficiently shown by the fact that the Unitarians were conspicuous in the development. Among the several theological tendencies in play, however, one may note a broadening stream of Eucharistic piety, visibly

Catholic Traditionalism 167

influenced by the Catholic Apostolic, Anglican, and Evangelical Catholic models. Not very much, in fact, has been added to their program in a century. Probably the most influential vehicle of the Evangelical Catholic program in the last third of the nineteenth century was the Church Service Society of the Church of Scotland, with its imitations in the Free Church and the American Presbyterians. Founded in 1865 to study the history of worship and prepare forms for the Church of Scotland, the Society had grown by the 1890's to include a third of the ministry of that church. Along with a series of half a dozen liturgical texts from Scottish history the Society published, first in 1867, its own book of suggested forms, called *Euchologion*. The work passed through some nine editions, of which at least four after the first represented significant revisions (1869, 1874, 1884, 1890). The compilers ranged widely, but their most characteristic immediate sources were the Catholic Apostolic liturgy, the American German Reformed *Order of Worship,* and the Anglican *Book of Common Prayer*. And by the agency of *Euchologion* these several tributaries were brought to bear on the first official service book of the Church of Scotland, *Prayers for Divine Service* (1923).

It would be possible to trace the increasing use of the fifth-century Latin pattern of the Christian year and of the Eucharistic prayer in these service books, especially since in some important cases, as of the Church of Scotland or of the Presbyterian Church in the U.S.A., or of the American Congregationalists, there have been now two or three generations of such liturgical commissions and their products. But the project does not seem very important. The merely traditionalist and antiquarian appropriation of Catholic forms and usages had its uses in the Reformed churches, but seems to have passed the point of diminishing returns. And just as the force of these Catholic influences has been, partly from success, losing its freshness, a very different type of Catholic thought on worship has made itself felt.

The reference, of course, is to the so-called "liturgical movement" which steadily gained strength in Roman Catholicism in the generation between World Wars and which achieved a remarkable triumph at the Second Vatican Council. This movement has effected something like a reversal of roles, the implications of which are still to be digested on the Protestant side. A deep pastoral concern and serious calling to mission to the world have replaced the defensive medievalism of Trent. The results, in many respects, have meant a startling convergence, at once with the early church and with the sixteenth-century Reformers. The new emphasis on Bible study, Biblical materials in worship, and the preached Word, while not always satisfactory to Protestant theologians, still stand as an inspiration and rebuke to much or most Protestant practice. The convergence is impressive on the normative complementarity of Eucharist and preached Word. The disgruntled reactionaries of the Council, on the other hand, and liturgical traditionalists since, have sounded like nothing so much as the nineteenth-century medievalist repristinators of the Protestant world, such as the Anglo-Catholic "ecclesiologists."

The mid-twentieth-century liturgical movement, however, is inconceivable without the antiquarian romanticism of the nineteenth century. It was the attempt to restore "correct" liturgical period pieces which built up a knowledge of the actual variety of history and in turn forced upon many the realization that there is no "correct" liturgical model, but that all vehicles of worship are composed of transient cultural forms shaped by the changing apprehensions of the gospel. The greater sophistication of our historical consciousness has made us aware of a much wider range of possibilities, and of the necessity for a more searching theological effort to identify and trans-

Catholic Traditionalism 169

late from one culture to another the affirmations and relations of Biblical religion. The awareness of historical relativity in the Roman Catholic liturgical movement has thus come to support the objections of the Reformers to any attempt at liturgical uniformity, since the unity of the church is not constituted by such matters.

We should not overstate the convergences. The basic disagreements of the sixteenth century on the nature of ministry and priesthood on the one hand, and on the propitiatory character of the sacramental act on the other, have not been resolved. Many contemporary theologians, Protestant and Catholic, find unexpected agreement across confessional lines as they seek more meaningful language and categories for the matters once debated under the rubrics of substance, real presence, and sacrifice. But the official polemic formulations and anathemas, as of the Council of Trent, remain in force.

Insofar, moreover, as the tendency of the Vatican Council revives in significant ways the intentions of the Reformers, it evokes the sobering inquiry as to why the latter had such qualified success. Even the best of liturgical scholarship, pastoral concern, theological power may not suffice today. All the resources of Protestantism and Roman Catholicism together will be strained to interpret and convey Biblical realities to the modern masses, dominated by the mentality of a technological industrialized age.

EPILOGUE:
HERITAGE AND VOCATION

THROUGH THE CHANGING FORMS OF ITS CORPORATE PRAISE the Reformed tradition has maintained certain characteristic emphases. This tradition has been distinctively Biblical, not so much in the sense of using Biblical materials in worship, or in insisting on the authority of Scripture, although it has done both, as in its affinity for the personalism of Biblical religion. While it has known such speculative metaphysicians as Jonathan Edwards and such contemplative mystics as Tersteegen, the dominant habit has rather been a "personal" view of God and of man and the drama of their relation, nurtured by the imagery and stories of Scripture.

This characteristic orientation in life and in worship may be defined in part by the contrast between two concepts, that of the "vision of God" and that of the "Kingdom of God." As Richard Niebuhr developed the theme, Roman Catholics have tended, in the train of Plato, Aristotle, and Plotinus, "to think of God as the eternal perfection of goodness, beauty and truth, to the vision of which the church led its children." Without rejecting this theory the Reformers more characteristically conceived of God (with Isaiah and Jeremiah and Jesus), as forceful reality or power, as Lord of Lords and King of Kings.

> To call the vision man's greatest good is to make contemplation . . . the final end of life; to put the sovereignty

of God in the first place is to make obedient activity superior to contemplation. . . . The principle of vision suggests that the perfection of the object seen is loved above all else; the principle of the kingdom indicates that the reality and power of the being commanding obedience are primarily regarded. The first term may also be interpreted to mean that the initiative lies with the one who seeks to see while the object is conceived as somehow at rest. . . . The term "kingdom of God" puts all the emphasis on the divine initiative.[77]

In the same vein but in slightly different terms Friedrich Heiler observed that "the two great lines of development, mysticism and the religion of revelation, constantly cross, separate and unite in the history of the Christian tradition." The Reformers marked a creative renewal of the prophetic devotion of Jeremiah, the psalmists, Jesus, and Paul. "The God of the mystic is the Infinite One, the *summum bonum,* in whom the mystic is completely absorbed; the God of prophetic prayer is the living Lord . . . the kind Father."[78] Despite the occasional Reformed contemplatives, the Reformed tradition as a whole has clearly been found emphatically, in terms of this comparison, on the side of the personalist and prophetic religion of revelation. Its worship has been characterized more by the forceful spontaneity of prophetic prayer than by the studied disciplines of mystical devotion.

This personalist apprehension of the divine has colored sensibility in art as well as worship. Each of the religious dispositions contrasted has its characteristic predilections and inhibitions in imaginative and aesthetic expression. Plastic representation may suggest the perfection of the object of contemplation, but has great difficulty with the summons to conscience, the voice of judgment or mercy. The Greek and Hindu readily turn to plastic representation or suggestion of the divine. But the Biblical injunction against graven images of the holy and righteous One

Epilogue: Heritage and Vocation   173

is no mere external legalism; it has a deep inner necessity. This reserve expresses itself in the themes and style of painting in Reformed communities, such as the Netherlands and England, in contrast to the religious painting of the Catholic Renaissance or Baroque. With church architecture, especially the disposition and decoration of interior space, the contrast is equally apparent.

The different emphases make themselves felt also in the interpretation of the Sacraments, depending on whether the terms of reference are primarily social and historical or natural and cosmic. The presence and character of the divine in the Bible are apprehended less in the vitalities and rhythms, or the prodigies and miracles, of the natural order, than in the human and historical manifestations of particular persons and events. The Hebrews of the Old Testament reinterpreted the rites and ceremonies of the nature religions around them with a primarily historical reference. Similarly the Reformed have not characteristically speculated like Tillich[79] about the symbolism of water in Baptism, or of the bread and wine of the Supper. These things are for them the stage properties of a sacred drama where the historical social meanings are the primary vehicle of divine visitation. The emphasis of the invocation at the Lord's Supper is less on the status of the bread and wine than on the hope "that He may dwell in us and we in Him." To some of "Catholic" orientation this seems inadequately "incarnational" theology. But is not anxiety about the status of the material elements of the Sacrament the consequence of another less personal view of God?

A contemporary Episcopalian writes of the sense of profound liberation experienced when he learned from the Benedictines of Maria Laach, as he might have learned from the Reformed theologians of Elizabethan Anglicanism, to focus his devotion, not on the objects on the Eucharistic table, but on the actions of the drama as representing the glorified Lord.[80] There may be significance, in this connection, to the tenacity with which the Reformed have maintained at the Lord's Supper the daring and dramatic ceremony of Jesus' own table action. However variously Communion has been received, at the table or in the pews, standing or sitting, the breaking and (sometimes) the pouring have been reenacted in full view of the congregation with awe-filled reverence. Those liturgies which have buried these symbolic actions out of sight are also the ones that have built up a preoccupation with the divine "substance" of the elements.

The role of social psychology in supporting this prophetic religious orientation should also be acknowledged. Every tradition is shaped under providence by constant interplay between the cultural milieu and the gospel. It is no denial of the Biblical personalism of the Reformed traditions to observe also its affinity for the psychology of the "bourgeois," the man without inherited status or privilege, whose individual distinction depends on his effort and capacity. This situation enforces a discipline and style of life setting a high value on independence, rational self-direction and restraint, initiative in action. To be sure, the Reformed churches have not always been middle-class or "capitalist," but over the centuries they have in most Western countries become predominantly identified with business, professional, and managerial groups. As such they have been conspicuous in the confrontation of Christianity with three of the most important tendencies of modern Western civilization, that toward constitutionalism and eventually democracy in politics, that toward economic rationalization and modern industry, and, in the intellectual sphere, the development of the sciences and the scientific world view. No other Christian tradition has been so intimately and so positively related to these developments. Sometimes the Reformed have accommodated themselves to secular pressure; at times they have to a degree disciplined and humanized these movements. But it has been

Epilogue: Heritage and Vocation

characteristic of these churches to live in this tension and to find here their vocation.

The worship of these churches has been the vehicle of a highly verbal, emotionally disciplined, intellectually critical mentality. It has never appealed widely to subliterate groups, either in the West, or on the mission field. But with its limitations and in part because of them, it has still an important calling in the science-dominated technological society where Christian liturgy and symbolism are so widely problematical. For the Reformed have always laid chief weight on what is now most crucial, the actualization of fully responsible personal existence before God.

NOTES

1. *Opera Calvini,* ed. by G. Baum, E. Cunitz, E. Ruess (Brunsvigae, 1884), XXVII. 407.
2. "The Supper is completely buried since it has been turned into the Mass, except that it is seen once a year, although in a mangled, halved, and mutilated form." *Calvin: Institutes of the Christian Religion,* ed. by John T. McNeill; tr. and indexed by Ford Lewis Battles (The Library of Christian Classics, The Westminster Press, 1960), IV. xviii. 20.
3. *Institutes,* II. viii. 5.
4. Christ has "given us a Table at which to feast, not an altar upon which to offer a victim; he has not consecrated priests to offer sacrifice, but ministers to distribute the sacred banquet" (*Institutes,* IV. xviii. 12).
4a. See Gregory Dix, *The Shape of the Liturgy* (London: Dacre Press, 1945), esp. Ch. IV.
5. Yves M. J. Congar, O.P., *Lay People in the Church,* tr. by D. Attwater (London: Bloomsbury Publishing Co., Ltd., 1957), pp. 123 f., 139.
6. Minucius Felix, *Octavius,* Ch. XXXII.
7. Luther, *Werke, Weimar Ausgabe,* 12.190.11.
8. *Canons and Decrees,* Session XXII, 1 and 3.
9. *Institutes,* IV. xvii. 44 (Allen translation). Much of what follows is a free commentary on the Calvinist service, available in English in B. Thompson, *Liturgies of the Western Church* (The World Publishing Company, Meridian Books, 1961), pp. 197–210.
10. Luther, *Tischreden* (Weimar: Hermann Böhlaus Nach-

folger, 1914), Vol. III, p. 673, as cited in T. H. L. Parker, *The Oracles of God* (London and Redhill: Lutterworth Press, 1947), p. 47.

11. *Opera Calvini*, XI. 41.

12. Cited by K. G. Fellerer, "Church Music and the Council of Trent," in *The Musical Quarterly*, Vol. XXXIX, No. 4 (1953), p. 585.

13. J. A. Froude, *Life and Letters of Erasmus* (Charles Scribner's Sons, 1894), pp. 122 f.

14. Cited in Fellerer, *loc. cit.*

15. O. Douen, *Clément Marot et le psautier Huguenot* (Paris: L'Imprimerie nationale, 1878–1879), Vol. II, pp. 350–377.

16. Cited in H. Y. Reyburn, *John Calvin* (London and New York: Hodder & Stoughton, Ltd., 1904), p. 85.

17. E. Mülhaupt, *Die Predigt Calvins* (Berlin and Leipzig: Walter de Gruyter & Co., 1931), pp. 12 f.

18. Douen, *op. cit.*, Vol. I, p. 9.

19. *Opera Calvini*, X. 213.

20. O. D. Watkins, *A History of Penance* (Longmans, Green & Co., Inc., 1920), Vol. I, pp. 494 f.

21. In Geneva the whole service was conducted from the pulpit most Sundays. When the Lord's Supper was to be celebrated, a table was brought in. See A. Biéler, *Architecture in Worship*, tr. by O. and D. Elliott (Edinburgh: Oliver & Boyd, Ltd., 1965), p. 58.

22. *Institutes*, IV. xvii. 46.

23. To Viret, Gotha MSS., p. 7, as cited in F. C. Schlosser, *Leben des ... Beza und ... Vermili* (Heidelberg, 1809), p. 451.

24. Reconciliation of enemies was effected at the Lord's Supper. See O. Farner, *Huldrych Zwingli's Verkundigung und ihre Ersten Früchte* (Zürich: Zwingli-Verlag, 1954), p. 517.

25. English translation of the text in Thompson, *op. cit.*, pp. 211–215.

26. *Ibid.*, p. 193, notes that this interpretation of the "Lift up your hearts" by the doctrine of the ascension stems from Farel.

27. *Institutes*, IV. xvii. 18.

28. *Ibid.*, IV. i. 3.

29. *Ibid.,* IV. xvii. 43.

30. Gregory Dix, *The Shape of the Liturgy* (London: Dacre Press, 1945), p. 633: "The real eucharistic action is for Calvin individual and internal, not corporate." This judgment, and the argument leading up to it, cannot be substantiated from the sources.

31. For the fullest account in English of the Strassburg development, although one to be used with caution, see W. D. Maxwell, *John Knox's Genevan Service Book, 1556* (Edinburgh and London: Oliver & Boyd, Ltd., 1931).

32. For Bucer's German and Calvin's French in parallel columns, see S. A. Hurlbut, *The Liturgy of the Church of Scotland* (The St. Alban Press, 1954), pp. 8–23. English translations are found in Thompson, *op. cit.,* pp. 167–210.

33. *Calvin's First Psalter,* ed. by R. R. Terry (London: Ernest Benn, Ltd., 1932), unfortunately disfigured by the editor's personal animosities.

34. J. Aymon, ed., *Tous les synodes nationaux des Églises reformées de France* (A La Haye: C. Delo, 1710), Vol. I, p. 181.

35. H. A. Wilson, ed., *The Order of the Communion, 1548* (London: 1908. Henry Bradshawe Society, Vol. 34).

36. For the texts, in addition to Thompson, *op. cit.,* see the Everyman's Library edition of *The First and Second Prayer Books of Edward VI* (1910).

37. See B. Van de Poll, *Martin Bucer's Liturgical Ideas* (Te Assen: Van Gorcum, 1954).

38. Nearly nine out of ten of the Sternhold and Hopkins tunes were in common meter.

39. See Maxwell and Hurlbut as cited above.

40. The Reformed familiarity with the metrical psalms probably rested even more on their systematic use on weekdays than on that on the Lord's Day.

41. Text in F. Schmidt-Clausing, *Zwingli als Liturgiker* (Göttingen: Vandenhoeck & Ruprecht, 1952), pp. 88–122.

42. English translation in Thompson, *op. cit.,* pp. 216–224.

43. H. Waldenmeier, *Die Entstehung der evangelischen Gottesdienstordnungen Süddeutschlands im Zeitalter der Reformation* (Leipzig: Verein für Reformationsgeschichte, 1916), p. 6.

44. English translation in Thompson, *op. cit.*, pp. 211–215. *Pace* H. Hageman, *Pulpit and Altar* (John Knox Press, 1962), Ch. I, the Basel service is probably a more typical and influential one than that of Zurich.

45. English translation in Thompson, *op. cit.*, pp. 149–156.

46. Text in Laski, *Opera,* ed. by A. Kuyper (Amsterdam and The Hague: Muller and M. Nijhoff, 1866), Vol. II, pp. 1–292, and excerpts in translation, B. Thompson, in *Theology and Life*, Vol. I (1958), pp. 106–112.

47. English translation by B. Thompson, in *Theology and Life*, Vol. VI (1963), pp. 49–67.

48. E. Gibbon, *Decline and Fall of the Roman Empire*, conclusion of the famous Ch. XVI.

49. *Institutes,* IV. x. 32.

50. Text in Thompson, *op. cit.*, pp. 311–341, and for the most helpful study of the subject of this chapter, see H. Davies, *The Worship of the English Puritans* (London: Dacre Press, 1948).

51. Cited in G. F. Nuttall, *The Holy Spirit in Puritan Faith and Experience* (Oxford: Basil Blackwell & Mott, Ltd., 1947), p. 66.

52. See W. Haller, *The Rise of Puritanism* (Columbia University Press, 1938), esp. Chs. I–IV.

53. See E. Morgan, *Visible Saints* (New York University Press, 1963).

54. Text in Thompson, *op. cit.*, pp. 345–371.

55. W. Lowrie, *Action in the Liturgy* (Philosophical Library, Inc., 1953), p. 220. Although described as "Calvin's prayer book," it is apparently the Westminster Directory which is here intended.

56. "I must tell you 'this great controversy' upon it [i.e., 'the lawfulness of set forms prescribed'] is raised only by yourselves and the Brownists, there being no divines, and no Reformed Churches that I know of, but do allow the lawful use of set forms of prayer . . . and do make use of such sometimes. . . . And I challenge you in all your reading to name one divine of note and orthodoxy that ever held set forms of prayer unlawful, excepting only Independents." T. Edwards, *Antapologia* (1644), pp. 98 f.

Notes 181

57. T. Leishman, ed., *The Westminster Directory* (Edinburgh: W. Blackwood and Sons, Ltd., 1901), p. 164.

58. W. Walker, "The Genesis of the Common Form of Public Worship in Our Non-Liturgical Churches," *Papers of the American Society of Church History*, Second Series, Vol. I (1913), p. 81.

59. Similarly in Massachusetts when the Brattle Street Church sought to restore the Lord's Prayer and the uncommented reading of Scripture, Increase Mather led the attack on such practices as "popish."

60. P. Miller, *Orthodoxy in Massachusetts 1630–1650* (Beacon Press, Inc., 1933), especially Ch. IV.

61. M. Goebel, *Geschichte des christlichen Lebens in der rheinisch-westphälischen evangelischen Kirche* (Coblenz: K. Bädeker, 1860), Vol. III, pp. 60–70.

62. E. Révész, J. S. Kováts, L. Ravasz, *Hungarian Protestantism* (Budapest: Bethlen Gábor Literary and Printing House Co., Ltd., 1927), p. 45.

63. J. J. Sessler, *Communal Pietism Among Early American Moravians* (Henry Holt and Company, 1933), p. 150.

64. *Ibid.*, p. 17.

65. B. L. Manning, *The Hymns of Wesley and Watts* (London: Epworth Press, 1942), p. 14. Manning also includes the canon of the Mass.

66. Text in Thompson, *op. cit.*, pp. 415–433.

67. A. Peaston, *The Prayer-Book Reform Movement in the XVIIIth Century* (Oxford: Basil Blackwell & Mott, Ltd., 1940).

68. As late as 1864 an American Presbyterian published a revision of the *Book of Common Prayer* according to those "Exceptions" as "the only Presbyterian liturgy that is either desirable or practicable." See C. W. Shields, *The Presbyterian Book of Common Prayer* (W. S. and A. Martien, 1864), p. 57.

69. C. H. Dodd, in N. Micklem, *Christian Worship* (Oxford: Clarendon Press, 1936), p. 79.

70. *Book of Worship for Free Churches* (Oxford University Press, 1948).

71. F. Heiler, *Prayer*, tr. by S. McComb (London: Oxford University Press, 1932), p. 109.

72. Cited in G. W. O. Addleshaw and F. Etchells, *The Archi-*

tectural Setting of Anglican Worship (London: Faber & Faber, Ltd., 1948), p. 219.

73. *A Liturgy, or Order of Christian Worship.*

74. P. Schaff, "The New Liturgy," in *Mercersburg Review*, 1858, pp. 218 f.

75. D. S. Schaff, *Life of Philip Schaff* (Charles Scribner's Sons, 1897), p. 178.

76. Eugène Bersier, the most distinguished French preacher of the 1870's and 1880's, was the most important figure. His *Église de l'Étoile* illustrated the Gothic architectural enthusiasm. His liturgy there included such ancient elements as the Kyrie, "Lamb of God," "Glory be to the Father," and the patristic dialogue and preface introducing the Eucharistic prayer. He led the prayers regularly from the holy table. His musical settings for the "Glory be to the Father," the Creed, and the Sanctus were not successful, and he had to settle for a reading of them by the minister, but he did get some congregational responses for the first time in the Huguenot church. He drew up the first history of French Reformed worship and drafted proposals in his *Projet de revision de la liturgie des Églises reformées de France* (1887). But his untimely death cut off his influence and he had few successors until well into the twentieth century.

77. H. R. Niebuhr, *The Kingdom of God in America* (Harper & Brothers, 1935), pp. 20 f.

78. Heiler, *op. cit.*, p. 119.

79. P. Tillich, "Nature and Sacrament," in *The Protestant Era*, tr. by J. L. Adams (The University of Chicago Press, 1948), pp. 94–114.

80. T. Wedel, "The Theology of the Liturgical Renewal," in *The Liturgical Renewal of the Church*, ed. by M. H. Shepherd, Jr. (Oxford University Press, 1960), p. 7.

INDEX

Absolution, 32, 42 f., 62, 72 f., 76 f., 81, 137
Action oder Bruch des Nachtmahls, 74
Addison, Joseph, 138
Agendbuchly. See Berne
Agnus Dei. See "Lamb of God"
Ainsworth's psalter, 95. See also Pilgrims
Altar, 18, 25–27, 51, 55, 63 f., 86, 146, 149 f., 157, 159–161, 165
Ambrose, 14
Ames, William, 95, 113, 119
Anabaptists, 12 f., 16, 20, 36 f., 73 f., 92 f., 97
Anglicanism. See England, Church of
Anglo-Catholicism, 28, 156, 158–163
Annoni, Jerome d', 120
Arianism, 125, 137, 139 f., 142
Arminianism, 109, 139, 142
Ascension, 79, 165
Augsburg: Diet of (1530), 52; order of, 53
Augustine, 14, 17, 97
Aulcunes Pseaulmes (1539), 57
Austin Friars, Church of the (London). See Strangers, Church of the
Awakening, 120, 129–133, 148 f.

Baird, C. W., 154
Baptism, 15, 22, 32, 41, 82, 91, 99, 119, 139, 144, 148, 151, 156, 159, 173; infant, 16, 24, 76, 93, 147
Baptists, Calvinistic, 97 f., 107, 109, 129, 139
Baptists, General or Arminian, 93–95
Baroque, 157, 160, 173
Barrow, Henry, 92 f.
Basel, 45, 53, 73–75, 120, 145
Baxter, Richard, 103
Bayly, Lewis, 114
Benedictines, 23, 36, 65, 173
Benedictus qui venit. See "Blessed be he who comes"
Berne, 53, 72, 120
Bersier, Eugène, 182n76
Beza, Theodore, 58 f.
Black rubric, 65
"Blessed be he who comes," 56
Bohemian Brethren, 73, 82 f., 121
Bohemian Confession (1575), 83
Bona, Cardinal, 157

Book of Common Order (Scotland), 36, 54, 68–70, 92, 98 f., 101, 154
Book of Common Prayer (England), 42, 44, 46, 48, 54, 60–67, 77, 88, 90–93, 101, 106 f., 109, 127, 129, 136–138, 142 f., 153 f., 159, 164 f., 167
Book of Common Worship (Presbyterian, U.S.A.), 166
Book of homilies, first (1547), 61
Book of Sports, 100
Bound, Nicholas, 100
Bourgeois, Louis, 36, 58
Bremen, 117 f., 146
Brenz, Johan, 86. See also Württemberg church order
Browne, Robert, 92 f.
Bucer, Martin, 42, 45, 50, 55–58, 60, 62, 68, 76, 78, 88, 91, 101; *Censura,* 64–66
Bullinger, Heinrich, 84

Calvin, John, 13–15, 17, 23, Ch. II *passim,* 56–60, 64 f., 68, 76, 78–83, 86–91, 97, 99, 101, 109, 154, 163 f.
Cambridge Camden Society, 160–162
Camisards, 120, 141
Campbell, Alexander, 148 f.
Campbell, Thomas, 148 f.
Cardale, John B., 156
Cartwright, Thomas, 92, 99
Catechism, Luther's *Small,* 15
Catechizing, 103, 113–115, 117 f., 132
Catholic Apostolic Church, 156–159, 164 f., 167
Ceremonial, 19, 49, 55, 63 f., 69 f., 74, 77, 82, 87 f., 90 f., 96, 106, 119 f., 149–151, 153, 157, 159, 161, 163

Chanting. See Plain song
Charles V, Emperor, 60 f., 75
Charleston, 144, 154
Christmas, 45, 74, 79, 153, 158, 165
Chrysostom, John, 14, 17
Church Service Society, 167
Clarke, Samuel, 137–139
Cologne, 60, 62 f., 66; *Consultation of,* 63. See also Hermann, Archbishop of Wied
Commandments, Ten, 16, 40, 43, 56 f., 63, 70–72, 76 f., 79, 81 f.
Communion, Holy: seasons, 148. See also Lord's Supper
Communion orders, medieval, 41, 46, 53, 56 f., 61 f., Ch. IV *passim*
Confession, general, 41–43, 59, 62, 70–73, 76–78, 104, 137, 144, 150, 154
Confirmation, 15, 119, 144
Congar, Yves, 26
Congregationalism, 47, 94–99, 107, 109, 114, 129–132, 139 f., 148–151, 166 f. See also Independents
Consubstantiation, 134
Continuous reading. See Preaching: in course
Conversion, 96 f., Ch. VI *passim*
Cotton, John, 96
Counter-Reformation, 83, 91, 109, 121, 156–160. See also Trent, Council of; Inquisition
Covenanters, Scottish, 108
Cox, Richard, 67
Cranmer, Archbishop Thomas, 27, 42, 58, 60–67, 75, 87, 92, 99, 106, 154
Creed, Apostles', 16, 34, 39, 41, 44, 70–82, 99, 105, 107, 137, 144, 146, 151

Index

Cromwell, Oliver, 107 f.
Cyprian, 14, 25

Dathenus, Peter, 36, 81
Dávid, Francis, 85
Debrecen, 84; Confession of, 85; Council of, 85
Decalogue. *See* Commandments, Ten
Deism, 139, 146
Deutsche Messe (1525), 54, 94
Didache, 13, 20, 45
Directory for Worship. *See* Westminster: Directory for Worship
Disciples of Christ, 148 f.
Discipline, 16–19, 45–47, 51, 57, 60, 91–93, 105, 115, 122, 158. *See also* Fencing of the Table; Tokens
Dix, Gregory, 179n30
Doddridge, Philip, 126, 139
Dort, Synod of (1619), 36, 82, 95, 113 f., 147
Douen, O., 34 f., 58
Durandus, G., 160
Dutch Reformed Church order, 43, 74 f., 81 f., 86, 90, 113–119, 147, 155; in U.S.A., 166

Easter, 15, 45, 74, 79, 123 f., 158, 165
Ebrard, J. H. A., 154
Ecclesiological Society, 160–162, 168
Edward VI, of England, 60 f., 65 f., 75, 81, 91
Edwards, Jonathan, 132, 171
Elders, 32, 77, 96, 105, 148, 158
Elizabeth, Queen of England, 33, 63, 65, 74, 90–92, 173
Emden, 61, 75, 81, 87

England, Church of, 12, 27, 31, 34, 47, 49, 60–67, 77, 86, Ch. V *passim*, 111, 122, 127–133, 136–142, 144, 149 f., 156, 159, 167, 173. *See also* Episcopal Church, Protestant; Anglo-Catholicism; *Book of Common Prayer*
Episcopal Church, Protestant (U.S.A.), 163, 173
Episcopalian Church in Scotland, 107
Erasmus, 34, 75
Eschatology, 105, 112, 118, 135, 156, 158
Eucharist. *See* Lord's Supper
Euchologion: Goar's, 157; Church Service Society, 167
Eutaxia, 154
Evangelical Catholicism, 156, 167
Evangelicalism, Ch. VI *passim*, 135, 138, 151 f., 163–165
Exceptions of 1661, Puritan, 129, 137

Farel, Guillaume, 56 f., 72 f., 76
Fencing of the Table, 46 f., 73, 80, 117. *See also* Discipline
Festivals of church year, 55, 79, 88, 100 f., 154, 165. *See also* Easter; Ascension; Pentecost; Christmas
Forbes, John, 95
Form of Prayers. See Forme des Prières Ecclésiastiques
Form und Gstalt. See Basel
Forma ac Ratio, 75–81
Forme des Prières Ecclésiastiques, 15, 54, 57, 143. *See* French Reformed Church order
Formula Missae (Luther's), 84
Franeker, 114, 118 f.

Frankenthal, 87
Frankfurt, 67 f., 75, 87 f., 92; church order, 53
Frederick the Pious, 78 f. See also Palatinate church order
French Reformed Church order, 35 f., 42 f., 55–60, 81 f., 85, 106, 109, 141 f., 144 f. See also Strassburg; Geneva; Bucer; Calvin

Gardiner, Bishop, 159
Gavantus, Bartolomeus, 157
Geleji Katona, István, 119
Gellert, C. F., 146
Geneva, 17, 29, 33, 43 f., 47, 53, 56–60, 65, 67–69, 72 f., 87, 92, 95, 100, 115, 142, 144, 154
German Reformed Church, 116–119, 145–147, in U.S.A., 156; 163–165. See also Palatinate church order; Evangelical Catholicism
Glas, John, 148
Gloria in Excelsis. See "Glory be to God on high"
Gloria Patri. See "Glory be to the Father"
"Glory be to the Father," 99, 107, 137, 150
"Glory be to God on high," 34, 56, 74, 143
Goar, Jacques, 157
Gönczi, Bishop György, 85
Gothic (church architecture), 160–162
Goudimel, Claude, 58
Grebel, Conrad, 74
Gregorian chant. See Plain song
Gregory the Great, Pope, 11, 14, 25
Grindal, Archbishop, 88, 91

"Hail Mary," 71
Halle, 121 f.
Harris, Howel, 130
Heidelberg Catechism, 78 f., 81, 85, 146
Heiler, Friedrich, 157, 172
Heltai, Gáspár, 84
Helvetic Confession (second), 85
Helwys, Thomas, 93
Henry VIII, of England, 65
Hermann, Archbishop of Wied, 60, 75. See also Cologne
Herrnhut, 121, 124
Hesse church order (1539), 60
Hesse-Cassel church order (1657), 146
Hippolytus' church order, 13, 15, 48
"Holy, holy, holy," 56, 63, 143, 150, 164
Hooker, Richard, 91
Hooper, John, 63, 75, 88
Hopkins, John, 67, 69
Hubmaier, Balthasar, 74
Huguenots. See French Reformed Church order
Hungarian Reformed Church, 42 f., 75, 80, 83–85, 90, 119 f.
Hussites, 82 f., 121
Huszár, Gál, 84 f.
Huycke, William, 63, 67
Hymnody, 36, 117–119, 123–128, 145–147, 162

Independents, 96, 99–107, 130. See also Congregationalism
Indulgences, 17, 24
Inquisition, 75, 87
Interim of 1547, 60, 75
Irenaeus, 25 f.
Irving, Edward, 156
Irvingites. See Catholic Apostolic Church

Index

James I, of England, 93, 98, 113
Jansenism, 119
Jebb, John, 161
Jerusalem, 19, 39
Jesus Christ, 16, 18–21, 24–26, 28, 37, 40, 45, 48 f., 122, 151, 171 f.
Jones, John, 137
Judaism, 19–21, 25 f.
Jülich, Cleves, Berg, and Mark, Synod of, 80
Justin, 21

Keserü Dajka, János, 119
King's Chapel (Boston), 138
Knox, John, 64 f., 67 f., 70, 77, 99; *Knox' Liturgy*, 68. See also *Book of Common Order*
Kózminek, Synod of (1555), 83
Kyrie Eleison, 43, 56, 63, 143

Labadie, Jean de, 115–117
"Lamb of God," 56
Lampe, F. A., 118
Lasco, John à, 33, 61, 64, 67, 70, 75–83, 96
Last Supper, 20, 64, 70, 74, 106
Latimer, Hugh, 27, 63
Laud, Archbishop, 95, 106, 112, 160
Lausanne, 73
Lecteurs. See Readers
Lectionary of church year, 55, 74, 79, 82, 86, 117, 119, 146, 150, 154, 167
Lecturing, 96, 102 f.
Lefèvre, Jacques, 30
"Lift up your hearts," 48, 56, 63, 73, 81, 143, 150, 154, 164
Lindsey, Theophilus, 138, 140
Lining-out of psalms, 59, 108, 127, 142

Liturgical movement (Roman Catholic), 13, 19, 168 f.
Lobwasser psalter, 36, 80, 85, 120
Locke, John, 148
Lodensteyn, Jodocus van, 115, 117 f.
London, 33, 61, 65, 75, 81, 87
"Lord, have mercy." See Kyrie Eleison
Lord's Prayer, 16, 41, 44, 70–72, 76, 78 f., 93, 105, 107 f., 115 f., 119, 153
Lord's Supper, 17–32, 40, 44–48, 50, 56, 59, 64, 68 f., 80, 91 f., 96, 105 f., 108 f., 115 f., 119, 122, 128 f., 139, 143 f., 146–150, 152, 156–159, 161, 164 f., 168, 173 f.
Louis XIV, 116
Luther, Martin, 13 f., 17, 27, 30–32, 44, 53 f., 66, 71, 73, 79, 94
Lutheranism, 12, 36, 43, 52, 61, 64, 67, 70, 78, 82 f., 85, 87, 117, 120 f., 135, 141, 144–147, 153, 163
Lutz, Samuel, 120

Manière et Fasson (1533), 56, 72, 73
Marburg, 53
Maria Laach, 173
Marot, Clement, 57 f.
Martène, Dom, 157
Mary, Queen of England, 65, 67, 75, 83
Mass, 15–18, 23 f., 27 f., 41, 51, Ch. III *passim*, 71, 74 f., 86, 119, 157, 159, 162, 165
Massachusetts Bay, 97, 114, 144
Meaux, 57; martyrs of, 39
Melanchthon, Philipp, 53, 60, 78, 83
Méliusz Juhász, Peter, 84 f.

Memorialism, 20, 64, 75, 77, 142, 148
Mérindol, Synod of, 73
Methodism, 124, 126–133, 148, 162, 166; Primitive, 131
Middelburg, 92, 113, 115 f.; Liturgy, 95
Milotai Nyilas, István, 85
Ministry, 12, 15, 17, 21–27, 33, 41, 169
Minucius Felix, 27
Missionary activity, 11, 13, 82, 114, 124, 131–133, 153, 163, 168, 175
Molnár, Albert Szenci, 85, 120
Montauban, Synod of, 58
Montbéliard, 53, 72, 88
Moravians, 120–124, 127, 133. See also Bohemian Brethren; Zinzendorf, Count von
Muhlenberg, Henry, 122
Music, church, 33–41, 161

Nantes, Edict of, 40
Neale, J. M., 159–163
Neander, Joachim, 117 f., 132
Nettesheim, Agrippa von, 33 f.
Neuchâtel, 53, 72, 142–144, 154
Nevin, J. W., 163
New Testament, 12 f., 19–25, 68, 70, 76, 104, 128, 143, 148
Newman, J. H., 159
Niebuhr, Richard, 171
Nîmes, 57
Nürnberg church order, 61 f.

Oecolampadius, 74
Old Testament, 21, 37 f., 68, 70, 76, 100, 104, 125, 158, 173
Olevianus, Caspar, 78
Olivétan, P. R., 30
Olney hymns, 125
Origen, 25 f.

Osiander, Andreas, 61
Osterwald, J. F., 142, 144
Oxford, 159

Palatinate church order, 43 ff., 74, 77–82, 85, 117 f., 145, 154
Palatinate tradition, 41, 44 f., 74, 81
Paul, 20, 22 f., 172
Penance, 16, 32. See also Discipline
Pentecost, 19, 45, 74, 79, 156, 158, 165
Perkins, William, 114
Pictet, B., 142
Pietism, 12, 50, 54, Ch. VI passim; 135, 147, 151, 154, 165
Pilgrims, 82, 95
Plain song, 35 f., 62, 154, 161
Plymouth Colony. See Pilgrims
Poland, Reformed Church of, 82 f.
Pons, 144
Prayers for Divine Service (1923), 167
Preaching, 17–21, 26, 29–33, 54, 88, 91, 96 f., 101–103, 108 f., 120, 123, 140, 143, 152, 158, 168; catechetical, 76 f., 79, 82, 147; expository, 30 f., 44, 55, 65, 72; in course, 66, 72, 74, 76, 78 f., 82, 101, 146, 165. See also Lecturing
Preaching order, medieval, 43, 53, 56 f., Ch. IV passim
Precisianism, 113
Preparatory service, 76 f., 80, 105, 147
Presbyterianism, 47, 98–110, 129, 132, 139–140, 148 f., 154–158, 162, 166 f.
Price, Richard, 147
Priesthood. See Ministry

Index

Priestley, Joseph, 147
Pronaus. See Preaching order, medieval
Prone. See Preaching order, medieval
Prophesying, 21 f., 33, 91–93, 96, 102, 115
Prussia, 118, 147, 164
Psalm Book, The (Scottish). See Book of Common Order
Psalmen, De CL, 81. See also Dathenus
Psalmody, metrical, 33–41, 58 f., 95 f., 108, 126 f., 155
Psalter, Huguenot. See *Pseaulmes de David*
Psalter, Strassburg, 55
Pseaulmes de David (1562), 38–41
Pullain, Valerand, 58, 60 f., 63, 67
Puritanism, 12, 54, 88, Ch. V *passim*, 111–116, 119, 123, 135 f., 139, 154, 159, 165. See also Exceptions of 1661, Puritan
Pusey, E. B., 159

Quakers, 98, 120
Quiñones, Cardinal, 65

Rákóczy, George I, 119
Readers, 69 f., 103, 143. See also Weekday services
Remonstrants, 113
Revivalism, 108, 130–133, 148 f.
Ridley, Nicholas, 27, 63
Ritualism, 159–163
Rousseau, J.-J., 144, 147

Sabbatarianism, 19 f., 100 f., 113–115, 132, 147

Sacraments, 16, 22–24, 31 f., 37, 144, 148, 164, 173
Sacrifice, 15, 19, 23–27, 63 f., 158, 164 f., 169
Sanctus. See "Holy, holy, holy"
Sandeman, Robert, 148
Sarapion, 13 f.
Savoy Confession, 96
Saxony, 15, 53, 66, 121
Schaff, Philip, 164
Schaffhausen, 53, 72
Scholte, 147
Schwarz, D., 55
Scotland, Church of, 86, 88, 98–108, 152, 154, 156, 165, 167
Scottish Prayer Book of 1637, 99
Sendomir, Consensus of (1570), 83, 121
Separatists, 12 f., 92–95, 97, 112, 116, 120. See also Anabaptists; Barrow; Browne; Labadie
Socinianism, 139, 144
Song of Simeon, 40, 51
Sternhold, Thomas, 66, 69
Stone, Barton, 148
Strangers, Church of the, 33, 61, 65, 75–77
Strassburg, 17, 32, 35, 41–46, 50, 54–60, 62 f., 65–67, 73, 75, 87, 92, 100, 104
Surgant, Johan, 71 f., 73. See also Preaching order, medieval
Sursum corda. See "Lift up your hearts"
Synagogue worship, 19–21
Szatmárnémeti, Council of (1646), 119

Taylor, Edward, 96
Taylor, John, 140
Teelinck, Willem 113 f.
Tennent, G., 122
Tersteegen, Gerhard, 171

Tertullian, 14
Tetrapolitan Confession, 52 f.
Thornton, Henry, 130
Tillich, P., 173
Tillotson, Archbishop John, 140
Tokens (Communion), 32, 105. *See also* Discipline
Tolnai Dali, János, 119
Toplady, Augustus, 123
Tracts, Oxford, 159
Transubstantiation, 24, 134, 157
Tremellius, 78
Trent, Council of, 13, 24, 27, 34, 60, 168 f.
Turretin, J. A., 142, 144
Tyndale, William, 30

Unitarianism, 84, Ch. VII *passim*, 166
Untereyck, Theodor, 117 f.
Ursinus, Zacharias, 78
Utenhove, Jan van, 75, 81
Utrecht, 115, 117 f., 147

Van Raalte, 147
Vatican Council, Second, 11, 13, 168 f.
Vestments, medieval, 63 f., 74, 88, 90, 157, 159, 162
Voet, Gisbert, 114, 117
Voltaire, F. M. A. de, 147
Voodlesers. *See* Readers

Wake, Archbishop William, 142
Waldegrave Liturgy, 92
Waldenses, 72 f.
Watts, Isaac, 37, 109, 125 f., 132, 139, 162
Weekday services, 18, 41, 59, 66, 70, 79, 103, 143; family worship, 103 f., 115, 130
Wesel, 88; Synod of (1568), 81
Wesley, Charles, 127, 162
Wesley, John, 111, 122, 127–131
Westminster: Assembly, 98–108; Confession, 96, 100 f.; Directory for Worship, 98–108, 129
Whitefield, George, 122, 129–132
Whittingham, William, 67 f.
Wilberforce, R. I., 159
Wilberforce, William, 130
Williams, David, 146
Wittenberg, 16, 54, 73, 84
Wolff, Christian, 147
Worms, 81
Württemberg church order, 53, 74, 78, 86

Zinzendorf, Count von, 121 f., 124, 130
Zollikofer, G. J., 145 f.
Zurich, 16, 33 f., 47, 52 f., 67, 72, 74–76, 84
Zwingli, Ulrich, 34, 45, 52, 64 f., 71–72, 74–75, 78, 82, 88, 151, 163

www.ingramcontent.com/pod-product-compliance
Lightning Source LLC
Chambersburg PA
CBHW071449150426
43191CB00008B/1284